Wisdom Sparks from the Soul
Contemplative Poetry

vanessa f. hurst, ms, cmc

Wildefyr Press
Louisville, Kentucky

Wildefyr Press Louisville, KY 40242

© 2025 Vanessa F. Hurst

Wildefyr Press is a trademark of Vanessa F. Hurst.
All rights reserved. No part of this book may be reproduced in any manner without the expressed written permission from the author.

Published in 2025. Printed in the USA

ISBN-13: 978-0-9908091-8-0

Special thanks to those who have foster the mystery and magic of poetry in my life. Mrs. Carolyn Altstadt, Peggy, Merlin, Lora, Bobbie, Linda, Annie, Angie — I know that I am forgetting someone! Oh, yeah! Moon Goddess Diana. If I've missed you, know that your name is written in invisible ink upon this page. Kudos to the ones that encouraged me to be a creator of beauty.

Many decades ago my seventh grade English teacher, Mrs. Altstadt, encouraged my writing of poetry. She called me the class poet. I have never forgotten her words or the feelings that they evoked. I was seen! I was a creative! That changed everything!

During the decades in between there and my entrance into social media, I wrote poetry for my own personal consumption. I kept this creative secret tucked away. There was a fear in sharing my poetry. What is I wasn't good enough? Those fears didn't stop poetry from speaking through me.

In the years that poetry has spoken through me, I have found that there is a mystery, a magic in poetry. Through melodious written word, a collage of images sparks forth inviting the writer and the reader into an extraordinary way of being. This is what I hope that my wisdom sparks do. Each poem offers a means of connecting heart and soul to lived experience. My hope is that it invites you to see the extraordinary hiding in plain sight.

Back to social media. There I discovered a new outlet. In the beginning, I anonymously shared my work. When I first published my poetry to Facebook, it was under an alias. In time, I became courageous enough to use my own name. Sharing on Facebook meant owning my inner poet as I shared her with the world.

What a nail biting experience! "What if I was trolled?" I worried. Well, that didn't happen. In time I got more comfortable with sharing the words that sparked from my core. Some poems that I thought weren't good, were fast favorites of others. Others that touched me, seemingly touched no one else. As the voices of those niggling worries lessened, I learned to create by listening to my soul and not worrying about how the words would land.

When I began posting on social media my morning poetic reflections, I wrote poems several times a week. Then, at the urging of my friend, Angie, I shared a morning reflection every day during lent in 2015. I've never stopped offering them daily since then. At some point, I began to call the memes I created for social media reflection arcs then they morphed into wisdom sparks. For me, they seemed to arc from my contemplative spirit and spark into the world.

Lest I get ahead of myself, you may be asking, "What is a wisdom spark?" A contemplative morsel to reflect upon at the beginning of the day. A thought to carry with you throughout your day. A poem to read once or reflect upon over and over again when the world just gets too uncertain, too messy, too untenable. I know what a wisdom spark is for me, I hope that you discover what it is for you.

Flash forward to now. I have gathered enough of, in my opinion, my "good" poems to create this book. Within it contains 367 poems or reflection arcs. One for each day of the year with an extra for that leap year day. Plus another because why not? I didn't deem every poem as suitable or good enough for this book. I spent time letting the poems from eight years sink into my being. I chose the ones that resonated with me. That sang themselves into this book. That arced across my being into the pages of this book. I used my intuitive spirit as the wisdom sparks chose themselves!

Simply put, each wisdom spark is a poem birthed from my intuition. It is a life lyric. A key that opens the gateway to the inner mystic. It offers an invitation to cross into liminal space and connect more deeply with yourself and the sacred.

Where do I get my inspiration? Some morning the words just tumble from my mind. Other times I find the words written in my journal. Sometimes they come through conversations with another person. No matter how they make themselves known, I believe that each wisdom spark resonates on the strands that connect me to the sacred and through the sacred to others and all of creation. These wisdom sparks are part of the contemplative web that creates my constellation of connections.

I've come to accept the mystery from which each wisdom spark makes itself known. I hope in the moments of reading, of allowing the wisdom spark to settle within you that you breathe into the mystery that connects your divine spark with the sacred, the All Spark. I also hope, if you feel called, that you create contemplative poetry for yourself.

As I chose the poetry, I realized that I wanted you, the reader, to experience the poetry with your mind, emotions, spirit, and body. I collaborated with my favorite artist, Merlin Lee, to create the artwork paired with each poem. These wisdom sparks — not all sparks are words! — are meant for you to run your fingers across, to recreate on a blank piece of paper or draw in sand. Use them and the poetry to lift you into the space of the sacred! Walk through that space throughout the day.

May wisdom spark from your soul,
Van(essa)

What to Do: How To Use the Poems and Images in this Book

You might be thinking or wondering out loud, "what do I do with this book?" It is not necessarily meant to be read cover-to-cover although that is perfectively okay. The book is meant to be experienced in whatever ways work for you.

Find that place of calm. Focus on your breathing. Flip open the book. Choose a wisdom spark. Read the words — out loud, silently. Let the words wash over you. Let them speak to you. Allow your fingers to trace, dance over the contemplative drawing that is paired with each wisdom spark.

Listen to your body/mind/spirit/heart response. Your response may be in a somatic feeling. An emotion. Words. Images. Percolations of your mind.

You might choose to walk as the words wash over you. Journal about them. Move to the words. There is no wrong way to contemplate with these wisdom sparks. There is only your way!

Through these wisdom sparks you are invited to engage life contemplatively. You might have noticed I use the word contemplative. What does that even mean? And, what does it mean to live contemplatively? For me, being contemplative begins with relationship: with yourself, others, the sacred, and all of creation.

- **Relationship with yourself**: This is about you. It's about loving each part of yourself: what you like, what you tolerate, what you ignore, what you want to never own. This is undoubtably the most important relationship. If you don't love yourself, how can you love anyone or anything else?
- **Relationship with others**: How you connect with family, friends, significant others, coworkers, acquaintances, strangers. These relationships ask us to be vulnerable, humble, and courageous with others. It is about being intimate in sharing who you are.
- **Relationship with all of creation**: This encompasses both the natural and human made worlds. Recognizing how you interact and what your stance is with each part of creation. What does respect mean for you? How do you live respectfully and reverently? These

relationships are found within the evolving answers.
- **Relationship with the sacred**: This is the thread that weaves your relationships into a cohesive whole. Through this relationship you amplify your ability to see the sacred in all. In a relationship with the sacred, you see the interconnectedness of all and live within that interconnectedness.

Back to the wisdom sparks. Breathe deeply of a spark's essence. Discover how it speaks to you…the unique message meant just for you. Let it flow into the cracks in your spirit, lift you beyond the mundane into the extraordinary contemplative world of mystery, call yourself home to you. In this journey allow grief, celebrate, and heal those parts of you long denied.

Table of Contents

a wild ride	1		no more, no less	37
that moment	2		shine your light	38
magic is	3		who you are not	39
practice	4		until the light dawns	40
balance in the uneven	5		today is the day	41
reflections of the soul	6		you cannot fail	42
a pure spark	7		say yes	43
whispers	8		a joyful heart	44
we are human	9		my wish	45
its really hard	10		don't forget	46
within the silence	11		the rhythm of my heart	47
monday morning blues	12		moon whispers	48
i want to be	13		a moon visitation	49
breathe	14		casting shadows	50
listen. see. touch.	15		be change	51
raindrops cascade	16		my passion	52
the master plan	17		a willow tree	53
the spirit of light	18		i am this	54
raku pottery	19		each teardrop	55
into the center	20		the most important person	56
compassion's erosion	21		no longer hiding	57
peace in your heart	22		the creeping dawn	58
heart cracks	23		forgiveness turned inward	59
the perfect life	24		something is growing	60
the winds of change	25		a new 'do	61
the echo of the moon	26		be the light	62
giving birth to your mystery	27		be your truth	63
trust in the journey	28		i want to heal	64
dawn is near	29		i want to let go	65
never-ending transformation	30		wake up!	66
the dream-spark	31		a flame, a spark, an ember	67
it's raining	32		what is right	68
breathe into the letting go	33		chasing suffering	69
what have you go to lose?	34		a journey through the tangles	70
now	35		nothing to prove	71
belief shatters	36		new growth	72
			a listening heart	73

full hands	74	unkinking words	113
like, dislike, life	75	within my heart	114
measuring life	76	soul sister warrior	115
the simple answer	77	resilience	116
goodbye, hello	78	is see you	117
love is	79	the predawn	118
the dark	80	into the tangle	119
this is it	81	don't stop believing	120
i am	82	show me	121
the moon as me	83	my true north	122
innocence awakens	84	look deeply	123
the time is now	85	not so different	124
no	86	i am me	125
when I believe	87	fear is	126
hope	88	free fall	127
a spirit soars	89	do you cry?	128
beginning of change	90	change is coming	129
a raging storm	91	making us whole	130
adrift	92	silence whispers	131
may you be	93	imperfections	132
banked in your soul	94	newness	133
you are invited	95	a quiet joy	134
simply amazing	96	we love	135
you are gift	97	soul essence	136
one drop	98	who you are	137
sometimes	99	arc into the world	138
the answer is here	100	who are you?	139
a single act	101	a wound so deep	140
no matter what	102	hope is	141
be the good	103	into the dawn	142
heal	104	a wildfire	143
your choice	105	signs	144
your lightness of being	106	your suffering	145
are you scared?	107	a fear stopper	146
i dance	108	a light so bright	147
freedom comes	109	the storm	148
what never was	110	in the wilderness	149
the great transformation	111	within you	150
what i know	112	freedom whispers	151

a renegade wind	152	start simple	191
no matter	153	the path of your dreams	192
wisdom's light	154	the scent of possibility	193
stillness	155	the truth within	194
echoing truth	156	each movement	195
the sun rises	157	a single raindrop	196
you are ready	158	an ill fit	197
the last puzzle piece	159	are you scared?	198
a sirocco wind	160	i love you enough	199
the cracks in your soul	161	boogiemen	200
inky blackness	162	unwrapping into the world	201
my cocoon	163	pulsing hope	202
on the ledge	164	our true nature	203
stand up	165	your soul song	204
my soul song	166	feeling is believing	205
not yet time	167	the night speaks	206
an internal response	168	breathe in the world	207
you are gift	169	life happens	208
open to magic	170	seeing-being	209
a reminder	171	a humanity reminder	210
an unexpected stem	172	the spirit yearns	211
a bird in the dark	173	the eyes of adversity	212
belonging	174	no matter	213
birthed from my truth	175	your beauty	214
welcome home	176	grief whispers	215
spiraling into life	177	a tsunami of change	216
sometimes i forget	178	inevitable	217
a fierce heart	179	never fear	218
take flight	180	no question	219
truth whispers	181	you are magic	220
a grace tattoo	182	be your power	221
the stars twinkle	183	lightning strikes	222
a welcome	184	world needs	223
deserving	185	without power	224
open your eyes	186	dawn whispers	225
grow your dream	187	within your soul	226
an expression of truth	188	kindling dreams	227
love awakens	189	i ride	228
your superpower	190	gather kindling	229

slipping through cracks	230	you are the world	269
stretch to the sky	231	the longest night	270
be the response	232	sacred calm	271
pilgrimage	233	yearning	272
so do i	234	a flickering candle	273
ride the thermal	235	seamlessly flow	274
find peace	236	believe	275
the night is quiet	237	birthing	276
a thin place	238	disappointment	277
the abyss of possibility	239	a barren land	278
my truth revealed	240	scatter hope	279
are you ready?	241	my absurd reaction	280
you thrive	242	unimaginable love	281
lit from within	243	a lotus blossom	282
seeds	244	too fast to hear	283
blind illusion	245	change is coming for you	284
a dream yearns	246	your birthright	285
mystery whispers	247	the way is simple	286
i am grace	248	freedom laughs	287
from the mud	249	i laughed	288
one more	250	A rejection, a correction	289
awakened inspiration	251	courage up	290
dark to light	252	your greatest act	291
grief's triad	253	be the breeze	292
chaos ricochet	254	accept responsibility	293
without	255	everlasting	294
a whisper of promise	256	renewal	295
enough	257	friend or foe	296
silence waits	258	don't	297
hope thrives	259	as close as letting go	298
the greatest gift	260	so bright	299
scatter seeds	261	you resist	300
no container	262	a fierce soul	301
like a fierce storm	263	your power	302
in the stillness	264	what stops you	303
be a beacon	265	it is you	304
arms wide open	266	be real	305
a power so great	267	embrace	306
a quiet hush	268	the end of the tunnel	307

no shame	308	not your foe	347
don't. give. up.	309	the power of dreams	348
the time is nigh	310	the whisper of free	349
open your soul	311	free to be	350
accept	312	really awake	351
saying no	313	bright enough	352
channel courage	314	believe in	353
the sand is shifting	315	into the unknown	354
greatness	316	the night is not over	355
bear witness	317	anyone but yourself	356
within chaos	318	it's not about	357
live fierce	319	no more detours	358
a way forward	320	becoming whole	359
a little bit lost	321	ask the question	360
untapped power	322	true to you	361
the moon casts light	323	no matter how dark	362
pointing toward	324	within the shards	363
five letters	325	may you	364
beginning anew	326	mystery	365
over my soul	327	i am expression	366
in yourself	328	night	367
living acceptance	329		
eyes open	330		
forgiveness	331		
winds of letting go	332		
echo of truth	333		
just because	334		
of magic	335		
conquer	336		
never enough	337		
got something	338		
two choices	339		
become the sky	340		
the winds blow	341		
uncertainty unraveled	342		
guiding me home	343		
set free	344		
shining within	345		
falling leaves	346		

a wild ride

intuition
a wild ride
into mystery,
a sprinkling
of magic,
a fierce song
of the heart,
a lullaby
calling you
home
to yourself

that moment

that moment
when i say,
i am ready;
i am not ready,
i am already there.

magic is

magic is
an unexpected illumination
a inner knowing
a catalyst of change
an unexpected transformation
a revelation of your inner most self

practice

practice is
everything.
everything
is practice

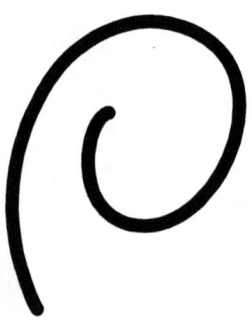

balance in the uneven

forgiveness
finds balance
in the uneven
calls forth our truth
forgets nothing
heals the ache
in our heart

reflections of the soul

violence is
an outward expression
of internal turmoil
nonviolence is
a reflection of
the beauty
of our soul

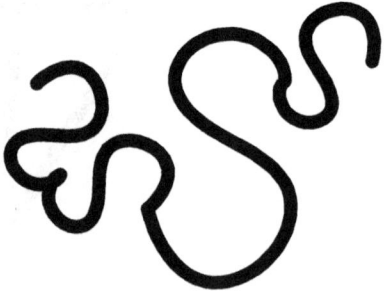

a pure spark

intuition is
a pure spark
illuminating the night
of uncertainty
guiding us
to our self.

whispers

i opened my eyes
what did I see?
my inner wisdom
whispering at me.

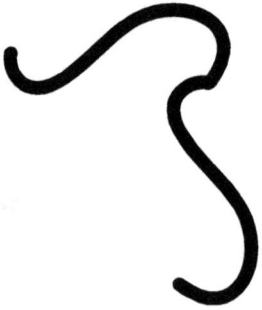

we are human

i do not agree with you
or you with me
doesn't mean
one of us
is wrong,
the other is right
it means
we are human

just because
i am hurt
by your actions
or you hurt by mine
doesn't mean
we are bad people
it means
we are human

just because
you do not fit
into my neat little box
or I do not fit into yours
doesn't mean
we cannot
coexist peacefully
by remembering
we are human

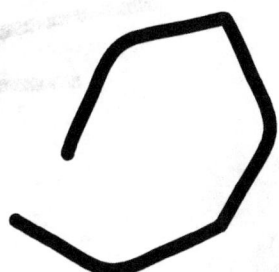

its really hard

someone said to me,
"compassion is really hard,"
and he was really right

within the silence

within the silence
illusion's shackles shattered
leaving me
free
to be
me

monday morning blues

monday morning blues
cannot compete
with sun's rays
chasing the darkness
across a lightening sky

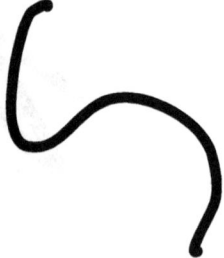

i want to be

i want
to be
like you.
she said.
i want
to be
like me, too.
and,
i want you
to be
like you.

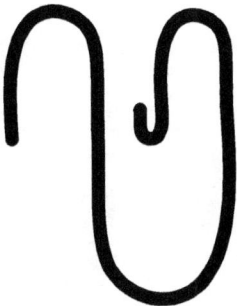

breathe

breathe
open to your beauty
breathe
rest in your core
breathe
be present to
your grace
breathe
hold on to peace
breathe

listen. see. touch.

listen
with your eyes
see
with your hands
touch
with your ears
speak
with your heart
dance
with your mind
your knowings
resonate
the message
of intuition

raindrops cascade

raindrops cascade
onto my soul
washing off my fears
the sun shines
evaporating
my monkey mind fog
the breeze dances
calming my emo being
opening me to peace
my heart opens
sparking the core
of who i am

the master plan

the master plan
is just a plan
don't cling
so tightly.
a ferocious beauty
beckons
from the wilds
of uncertainty.
breathe into
the rhythm
of its spontaneity,
live your impossible possible

the spirit of light

the spirit of light
bursts into the world
sparking wisdom
igniting love
flaring peace

the spirit of light
rests in the heart
eases the mind
relieves tension
emboldens the soul

i am the spirit of light
i am the presence of life
i am the keeper of wisdom
i am the warrior of peace
i am you.

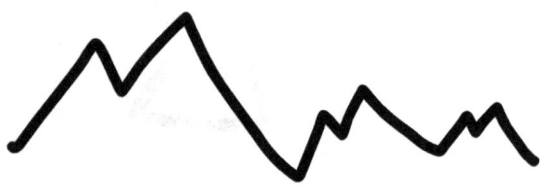

raku pottery

my heart
is raku pottery
cracked by suffering
healed by
compassion-gold

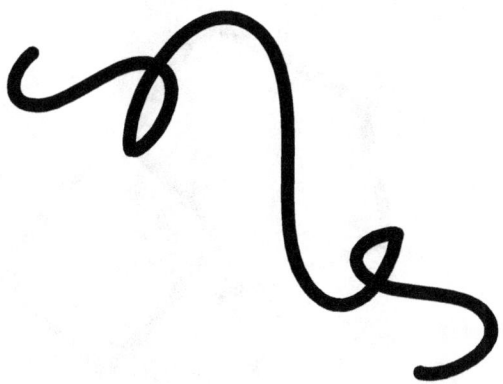

into the center

breathe into the center
ignite your spark
believe the impossible
shining through
the cracks of possibility

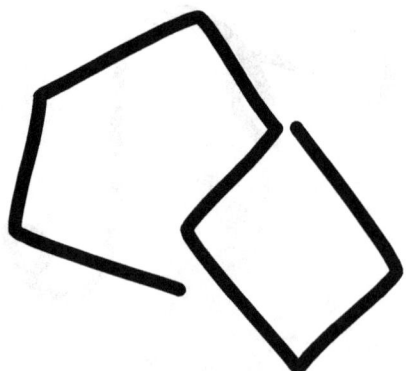

compassion's erosion

my mom used to say,
"kill them with kindness."
Instead, I think
I will erode
them with compassion!"

peace in your heart

 without peace
in your heart
you can never be
peace in the world.

heart cracks

those cracks
in my heart are
scars of suffering
badges of courage
openings for healing
pathways of compassion

those cracks
in my heart are
a roadmap
of transformation —
mine
and yours

the perfect life

stop protecting
your so-called-perfect-life.
breathe in
the wild, wonderful,
totally petrifying
world of possibility.
you will not be sorry.

the winds of change

the winds of change
rattle the doorknob
don't open the door!

the winds of change
seep through the cracks
burrow into your blanket!

the winds of change
whistle a melancholy tune
close your ears!

the winds of change
sing resistance is futile
i will not be denied

the winds of change
whistle, open the window
breath in my change
be the change

the echo of the moon

the moon
in the sky
of our soul
illuminates
the shadows
of our spirit

the moon's echo
awakens
the mystery
at our core

the moon's
waxing & waning
brings us home
to ourself

giving birth to your mystery

the night
lengthens,
the light
in your soul
grows.
prepare
to give birth
to your mystery.

trust in the journey

life is
an adventure —
a curious,
winding journey
beckoning us
to where
we need to be.
trust
in the journey

dawn is near

the night
is long
the shadows
grow
illusions
creep
shine
your truth
live
your light
for dawn
is near

never-ending transformation

the past
not a dress rehearsal
but a repository
of life learnings,
challenges met
an arena in which
you meet yourself
in each moment.
a never ending
transformation,
a realization
of who you are

the dream-spark

clinging tightly
to a dream,
the rest of your life
cannot breathe.
let go
breathe deeply
into the dream-spark
at your core

it's raining

it's raining
washing away
the grime
revealing
forgotten beauty
splattering
change upon
a thirsty world

breathe into the letting go

we cannot hold
on to anything.
all we can do
is open our hands
breathing into
the letting go

what have you go to lose?

believe.
trust.
love.
what have
you got
to lose?

now

now is not the time
to hide away
to hunker down
to hibernate
to take just one more nap

now is the time
to let go of fear
to stand in your power
to be courageous
to live curiously
to dare to be

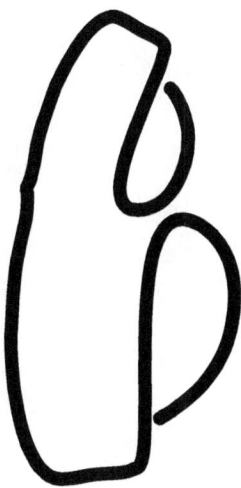

belief shatters

belief in why not
shatters the mundane
brightens colors,
sharpens joy,
sweetens love.
assures possibility

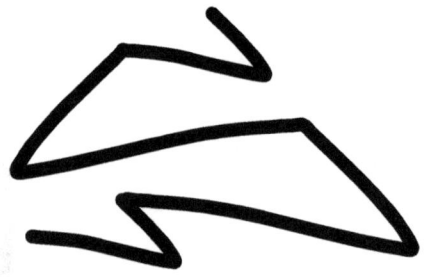

no more, no less

your projection
into the world
is no more,
no less
than the beauty
of your soul.

shine your light

your purpose
is no more,
no less
than to shine
your light
that is all,
that is enough.

who you are not

let go
of the chains
that bind you
to who
you are not

until the light dawns

the tendrils of dark
wrap themselves
around you
not to strangle
your hope
but to hold
you up
until the light
dawns

today is the day

today
is the day!
go big!
live fully!
love all!
shine!
today
is the day!
go big!
be
who you are.

you cannot fail

within you
is a power
so great
a light
so bright
a grace
so profound
— you cannot fail.

say yes

say yes.
whisper it.
shout it.
ride the wind
of joy
echoing in
the great nothingness
of your soul

say yes.
whisper it.
shout it.
those three letters
tilt your world
bringing
transformation.

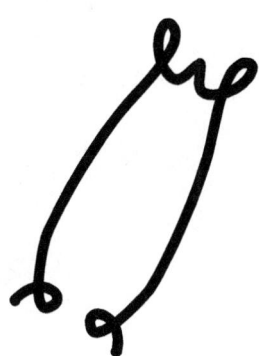

a joyful heart

a joyful heart
is a magnet
for limitless possibility.

my wish

my wish for you:
to know
the joy
in each heartbeat
to know
the dance
in each step
to know
the peace
in each breath
to know
the wonder
in each glance
to know
the presence
of the sacred
flaring
from your core

don't forget

don't spend
so much time
shining your light
that you forget
you are a shining light.

the rhythm of my heart

i dance
because
my feet
cannot stop
from moving
to the rhythm
of my heart

moon whispers

the moon
wanes
whispering
let go
of what
holds you back

the moon
waxes
shouting
embrace miracles
of movement

a moon visitation

last night
the moon visited
shining her light
filling my room
washing across my bed
waking me to my power

casting shadows

life is
like the moon
sometimes full,
sometimes waxing,
sometimes waning,
sometimes new
casting shadows
on a changing landscape

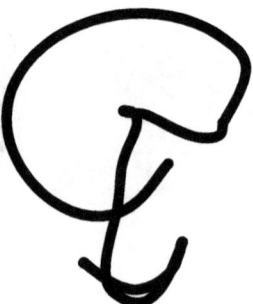

be change

be a change agent
believing in impossibilities
an imperfect rebel
committing to a cause
a daring windrider
leaping into currents uncertain
a wounded healer
walking between worlds
be change

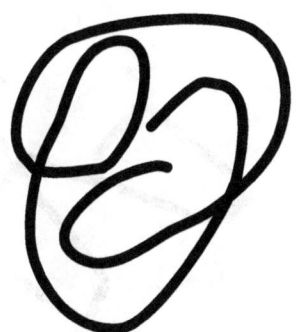

my passion

the world
is on fire
my passion
can temper
the flames
or ignite
even greater destruction
my passion,
my choice

a willow tree

a willow tree
bends
only so far
before
it breaks

i am this

i don't
"got this"
I am
this

each teardrop

each teardrop
erodes suffering,
revealing a trail
of possibility.

the most important person

love yourself
you are
the most
important person
in your life.

no longer hiding

i can
no longer
hide
who i am

the creeping dawn

the creeping dawn
shines light
upon the beauty
of my soul.
i breathe in
the grace
that i am.

forgiveness turned inward

forgiveness is
compassion
turned inward
you forgive
to heal
your woundedness

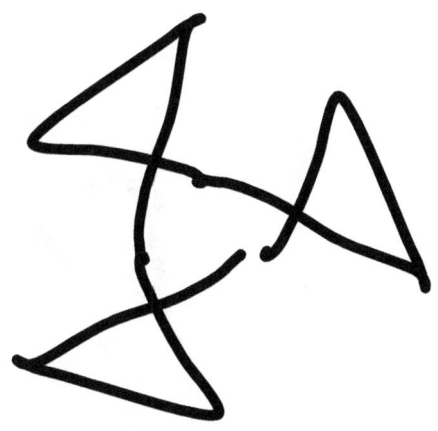

something is growing

no matter
how arid the land,
keep throwing seeds,
keep cultivating the soil
keep watering seedlings
have patience
something is growing
even if you cannot see it.

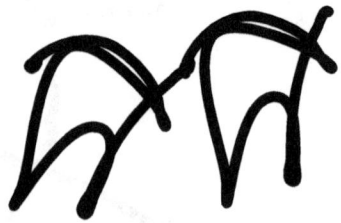

a new 'do

the winds
of change
whip through
my soul
messing it
into a new 'do.
i like it.

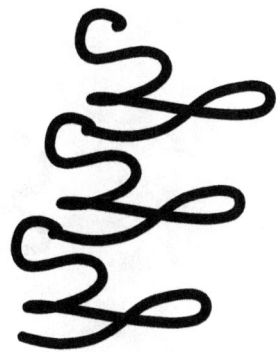

be the light

be the light
that illuminates
yourself
shine the light
for others
to find you.

be your truth

live in paradox
be the contradiction
shift the paradigm
dance in the margins
be your truth

i want to heal

i want to
embrace the hurt
befriend the sorrow
release the suffering
i want to
forgive you.
in the forgiveness
i want to
heal myself

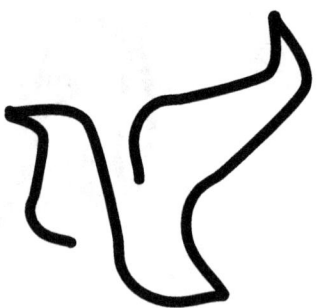

i want to let go

i want
to let go
stop picking
at scabs
be gentle
with my bruised heart
i want to forgive you

i want
my head
to relinquish control
of my heart
to soothe
the riot
in my body
i want to forgive you

i want
my spirit
to connect
my head, heart, body
to soar free
above my judgment
as I forgive you

i want
my suffering
to stop pooling
in the marrow
of my bones
to dissipate
into compassion
as I forgive you

i want
my compassion
to turn inward
to spiral outward
as I forgive you

wake up!

wake up!
act
if not you,
then who?

a flame, a spark, an ember

in the darkness
a flame dances
casting shadows
upon a scarred heart

in the rising light
a spark flies
illuminating
a hope, a healing
on a crooked path

in the light of day
a fire banks
sustaining
compassion
within the spirit

in the twilight
an ember glows
filling the self
with courage & daring

in the darkness
a light flickers
guidance
through the shadows

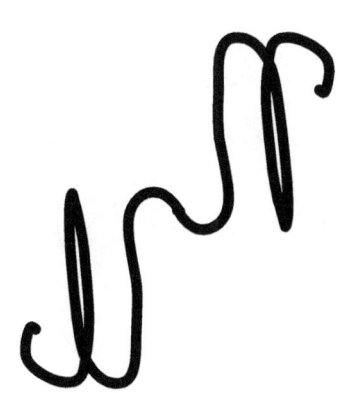

what is right

always doing
what is right is
in your best interest.
always.

chasing suffering

be the light
that chases
the suffering
from shadows

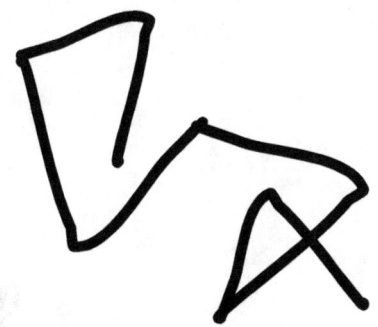

a journey through the tangles

life is
a jungle
of tangles,
uncertainty,
untold wonders
a journey navigated
with inner wisdom.

nothing to prove

be
yourself.
shine
your light.
reflect
your true self
you
have nothing
to prove.

new growth

may the wildfire
of your spirit
burn away
the underbrush
of uncertainty
in your soul
readying the soil
for growing
stems of
transformation

a listening heart

listen
with the ear
of your heart
speak
with the tongue
of your soul
live
from the spark
at your core

full hands

my hands
may be full
but there is
always room
in my heart
to listen.

like, dislike, life

do not take
so personally
the actions
of another
there will
always be
someone
who does not
like you
there will
always be
someone
you do not like

measuring life

life is not
measured
by fair.
life is
measured
by well lived.

the simple answer

the answer
is simple.
live from
your heart.
be who
you are.

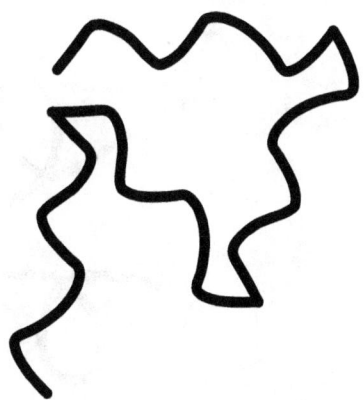

goodbye, hello

embrace
each good bye
with a joyful hello
bless
the ending
to welcome
the beginning

love is

love is
not an obligation
love is
a wild, welcoming
an embrace
of wholeness.

the dark

the dark is not
a scary place
the dark is
a treasure trove
of challenges,
a learning
of lessons.
the dark isn't
a warm, cozy place
it is an edgy place of
the ultimate
transformation.

this is it

no more waiting.
no more yearning.
this is it.
open the door.
step through.
believe
this is it.

i am

i am
a sharer of grace
a light flickering
through my dark
a healer,
a crisscross
of scars
a fierce lover
i am
simply me

the moon as me

the moon waxes
as do i
growing into fullness,
abundance,
brightness,
realness.

the moon wanes
as do i
letting go
what need not be,
light hidden
but not gone.

innocence awakens

at the beginning
of each day
innocence awakens,
whispering,
"believe in my beauty."

the time is now

do not doubt
breathe
in possibility
be humble,
vulnerable
all is well
all is coming
together
this is it
the time is now

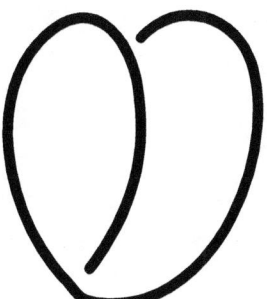

no

the most powerful word
you may utter
is "no."

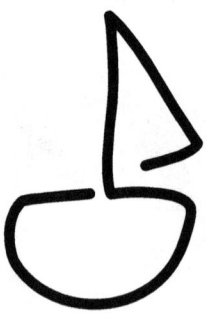

when I believe

when I believe
in my goodness
when I accept
who I am
when I recognize
my light
i stand
in my power
shine my message
brightly into
the world

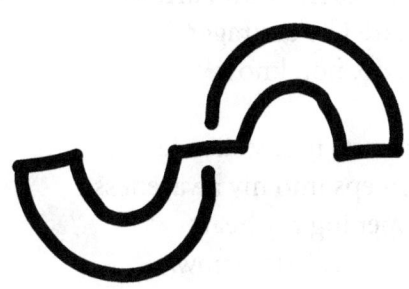

hope

hope
that four letter word
i am afraid to be
what does that mean
i. do. not. know.

it opens vistas
makes me wonder
can have more?
i. do. not. know.

it shines a light
opens me to potentials
are they really possible?
i. do. not. know.

it touches my heart
casts light in my dark
will despair leave?
i. do. not. know.

it is a fleeting companion
graces me with curiosity
dare i be courage?
i. do. not. know.

it rests in my silence
creeps into my awareness
opening my heart
maybe. i. do. know.

a spirit soars

leaping into
wild.
wonderful.
passionate.
free.
my spirit soars

beginning of change

one day
i woke
realizing the world
didn't need
to change;
i did.
that was
the beginning
of my truth song

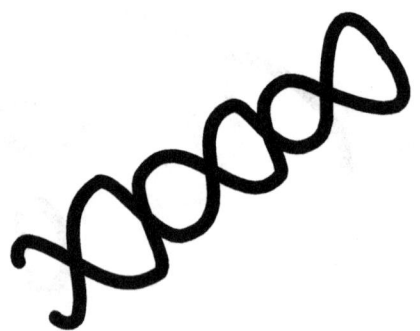

a raging storm

the storm
rages within
eroding illusions
clearing the way
baring the real
welcoming you home

adrift

adrift in turmoil
swimming
against the current
wishing for a boat
being swept into
the whirlpool
of my dreams
that's life

may you be

may you be free
may you embrace
the innocence
of your heart
may the world
not change you
may you
change the world

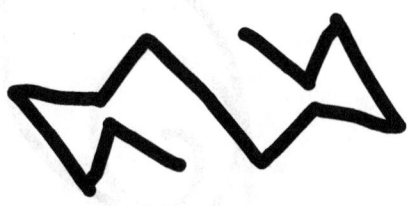

banked in your soul

the light you see
is not the coming dawn
it is the ember of hope
banked in your soul

you are invited

you are invited
again and again
into celebration
to reflect the beauty
of your soul
onto the world

simply amazing

the world is
simply amazing
so are you.
don't give up
share your strength
smile your smile
realize your core
gift your grace.
the world is
simply amazing
because of you.

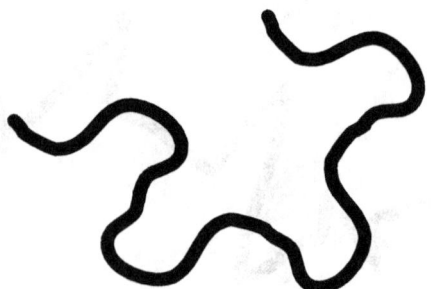

you are gift

you are gift.
without your grace
without your light
without your presence
the world would shine
less bright.
never forget
you are gift.

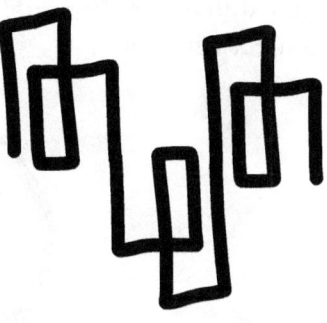

one drop

i am one drop
in a sea
of forever
becoming
the sea's rhythm
as i swim
from here to there

i am one drop
in a torrential downpour
plummeting to the earth
as i quench drought's thirst

i am one drop
among many other drops
making a difference
as i connect with you

sometimes

sometimes
i am so stuck
in what
i want to see,
what i want
to believe,
that i lose sight
of what is
really true
of who
i really am

the answer is here

open
the eyes
of your soul
the ears
of your heart
listen
the answer
is here.

a single act

in a single act
of kindness
you find yourself

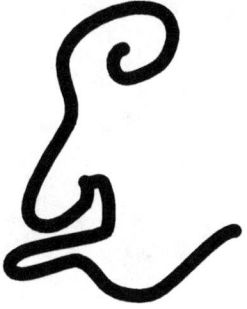

no matter what

i am the voice
nudging you to
unfurl your wings,
take flight,
live your life
no matter what

be the good

be the good.
the world can be
a dark, scary place.
be the good.
it powers you
through the dankness
be the good
it amplifies your grace
be the good.

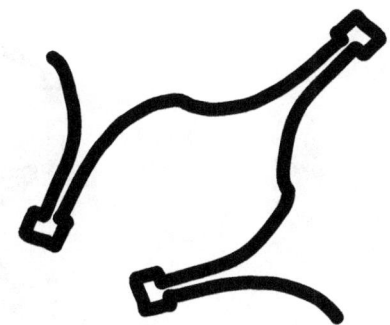

heal

heal
with laughter
with tears
with eyes
with hands
heal
with your being

your choice

will you live
with your whole heart
hide in
the shadows,
or be stuck
somewhere in-the-between?
it is yours to choose

your lightness of being

sit in the dark moon
breathe in potential
sit in the full moon
breathe in possibility
sit in the rising sun
breathe out intention
sit in the setting sun
breathe out resolution
sit in the moment
breathe in,
breathe out
be your lightness of being

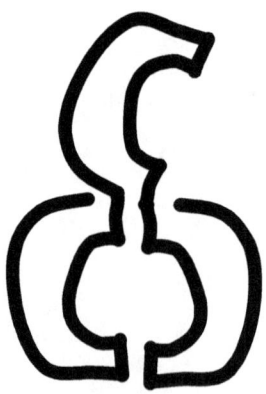

are you scared?

are you scared?
so am i.
fear can
paralyze or free
are you scared?
so am i.
let's join
point of light
to point of light,
confront
the darkness
you and i
are you scared?
so am I.
together
our courage
becomes hope.

i dance

i dance
because
my feet
will not
stop singing
soul purpose.

freedom comes

don't cling
so tight
freedom comes
when you soar

what never was

you never discover
what can be
when you cling
to what never was.

the great transformation

we are
compassion
rebels
living
during
the great
transformation

we are
compassion
sparks
shining with
courage,
curious daring

we are
compassion
alchemists
transmuting
lead to gold

we are
compassion
in action
knowing we are
the change

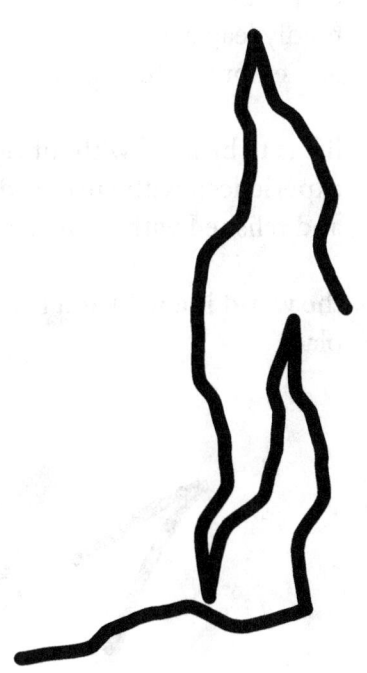

what i know

what I know
boxes are best used
for storage and moving
not ideas and people
fear is best experienced
in small doses
and reserved for the known

we are meant to dance
on the head of a pin,
boldly leap across great chasms
and embrace the raging fire within

life is to be lived without reservation
experienced with curious daring
and relished with unbridled courage

the world is a wild and beautiful
place

unkinking words

"you have a lot to share," she said.
i exhaled, "yes, I do,"
those words unkinked
the hitch in my soul.

within my heart

within my heart
is a blemish,
a sore spot,
rubbed raw
from suffering.

within my heart
is a raging compassion fire
enveloping the blemish
with hope, trust, courage

within my heart
is understanding
of the beauty
of my soul.

within my heart
is the echo
of my truth
simply, complicated me

soul sister warrior

i am a compassion warrior
the walking wounded
whose heart has been broken,
bruised, and battered

i am the wounded healer
who through the grace of
compassion
heals again and again and again

i am the heart and soul of
compassion
who reaches out to you
not as healer
but as soul sister warrior

i am compassion's presence
i am you
you are me
together we are compassion

resilience

have the resilience
to confront
your wounds
have the courage
to forgive
have the daring
to begin anew.

is see you

i see. i see you —
the external,
the internal.
the you crying desperately
to be seen,
to be heard,
to be touched.
i see you as intimate stranger

i see. i see you —
the happiness, the joy ,
reflected
in your eyes
the deep, sorrowful
wounds
you valiantly hide
i see you as fellow sojourner

i see. i see you —
not the scars, the wounds,
the other
from whom
i run and hide
i see you as a flower
growing amongst
other flowers
in the ground
of my being

and, when i see you
and you see me
illusions vanish
the chasm of
separateness disappears
revealing communion
i see you walking with me

the predawn

in predawn dark
magic twines between
what if and what could be
in predawn stillness
mystery weaves between
fear and hope
in predawn anticipation
i slip to the edge,
unfurl my wings
leap into possibility

into the tangle

breathe
into the tangle
follow one strand
to another
to another
its not over yet
let the knots
loosen
slip between
reweave
find your truth
breathe into hope

don't stop believing

don't stop believing
in the beauty
of your soul
don't stop believing
in the courage
of your heart
don't stop believing
in the curiosity
of your mind
don't stop believing
in the resilience
of your body
don't stop believing
in you

show me

show me
a different way
as the light shines through
the cracks of this box
i find myself in

show me
a different way
as the gale blows
one side down
then the other
then the other
and the last one falls.

show me
a different way
as i laugh with joy
knowing my eyes
were closed
to something so simple.

show me a
different way
that I may be
true to myself.
show me
this way

my true north

i am
imperfect
i have
small blemishes,
slashing scars
some imperfections
visible
some tucked into
the recesses
of my soul
i am imperfect
those imperfections
navigate me
to my truth

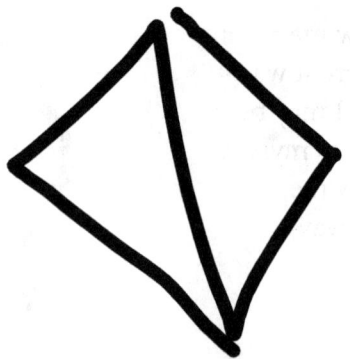

look deeply

the full moon
casts shadows
shifts,
twists,
warps
the landscape.
i look deeply
into the shadows
to what is.

not so different

we are
not so different,
you and i.
both our hearts
beat the same tattoo
of life.

i am me

i am a warrior
fiercely independent
wildly free
walker between worlds
shifter of paradigms
sharer of possibility
i am me

fear is

fear is
a flash flood
of uncertainty
leaving debris
of the unknown.
fear is
an invitation
to courageous action

free fall

free fall
into
the messiness
of life
forgive
your self.
forgive
others.
find
meaning
within
forgiveness

do you cry?

do you cry?
tears of sorrow.
tears of joy.
tears that cleanse.
tears that propel you
beyond yourself
do you cry?
i do.

change is coming

change
is coming.
don't break.
be a willow.
bend
into the winds.
stand
in your power.
let the fear
slip from
your branches.
change
is coming.
you
are ready.

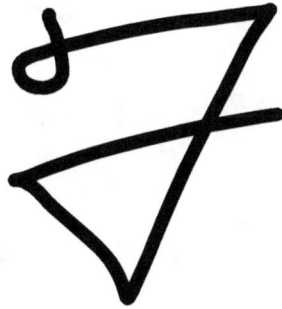

making us whole

dark,
light,
in between
weaving together
to make us whole
this is our power

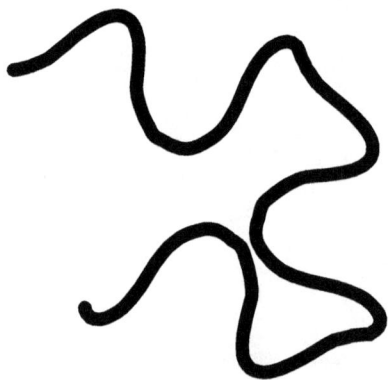

silence whispers

in the quiet
of the night,
silence whispers
an invitation
into the mystery
of being.

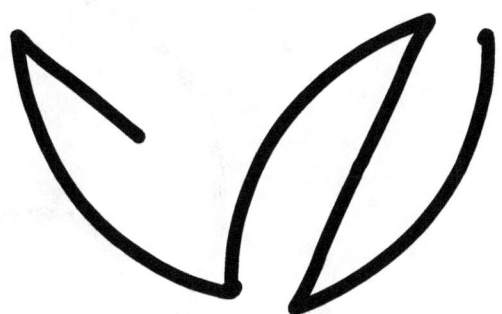

imperfections

the uncertainty
in the world
doesn't prevent us
from living.
the fear
of our imperfections
does.

newness

we can cringe
in the cold,
blustery wind
or
we can feel
the power
of the wind
nudging us
into newness

a quiet joy

a quiet joy
is found
in each moment
of gratitude.

we love

we love
not because
someone
is deserving
but because
not to love
is to deny
who we are.

soul essence

to love
is to share
the essence
of our soul.

who you are

live simply:
learn
who you are
love
who you are
be
who you are
share
who you are

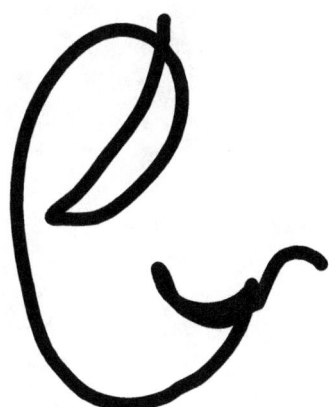

arc into the world

be a spark
that ignites
your heart
be a torch
that sparks
others
be a flare
that arcs
into the world

who are you?

who are you?
the light,
the dark
the joy,
the sorrow
the messy,
the pristine
who are you?
the light
that shines
from your core
that is
who
you are

a wound so deep

within my heart
is a wound
so deep
the only thing
seeping from it
is compassion.

hope is

hope is
honoring
opportunities
with positive
expectations.

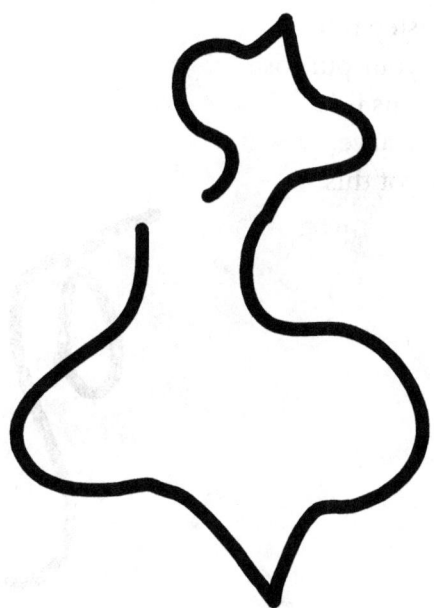

into the dawn

this is it.
what you
have been
waiting for
is here.
listen.
peer into
the dawn.
step into
your purpose.
this is it.
you've
got this.

a wildfire

be the person
that sparks
a wildfire of compassion
into the world.

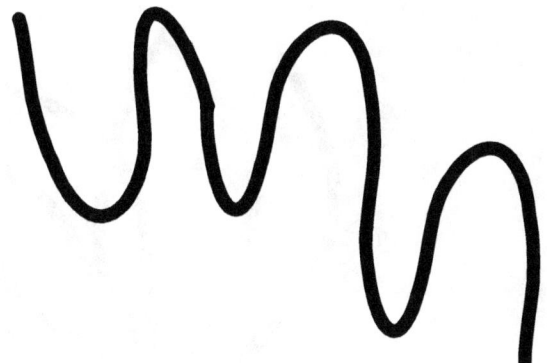

signs

it's time.
could the signs
be any clearer?

your suffering

may your suffering
be a healing balm
for your heart.
may your suffering
be a catalyst
for transformation.
may your suffering
be the compost
from which
you grow.

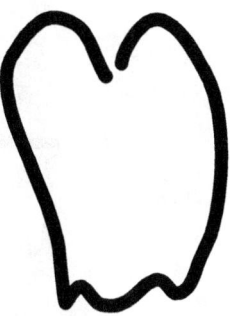

a fear stopper

courage is
a fear stopper

courage is
the power of belief

courage is
a game changer

courage is
at your core

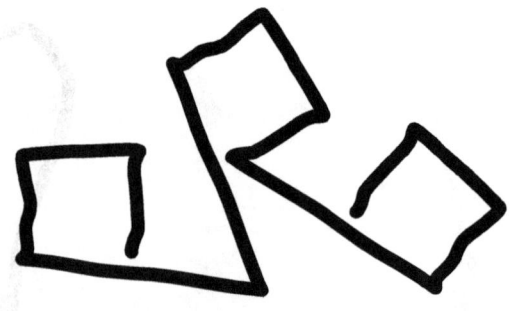

a light so bright

within you
is a light
so bright
that you cannot help
but share it
with the world.

the storm

the storm is
not coming.
it is here.
gather the turmoil
raging around you.
transmute to peace
step into your power.
act.
transform.
that storm?
it is you.

in the wilderness

in the wilderness
of my heart
are brambles
that tear at illusions,
in the wilderness
of my soul
are feral courage seeds
growing through the holes
sharing my true self

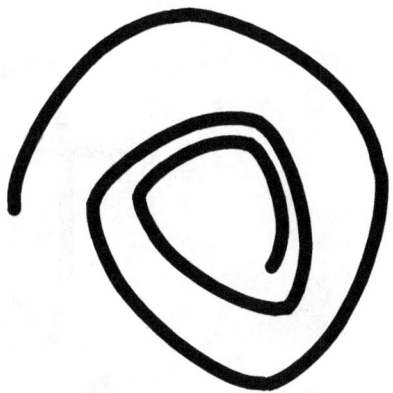

within you

within you
is a sun
so fierce
it melts away
the icicles
of fear
warms
the courage
in your heart
lights
the path
of transformation

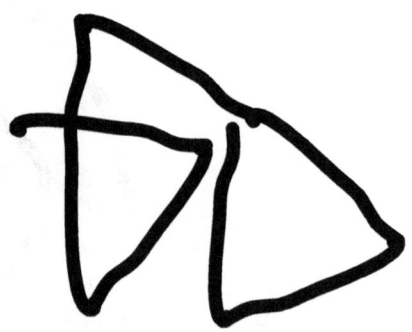

freedom whispers

"free,"
the mountain whispered at me
free to scale peaks of fear
free to forge paths of courage

"i am free,"
i shouted to the mountain
and, it echoed back to me.

a renegade wind

a renegade wind
floats in the air
awakening
your rebel spirit
blowing away
stale uncertainty
lifting you
higher and higher
upon the thermals
of your dreams

no matter

no matter
how dark the night,
no matter
how small the flame,
a light flickers
in the center
of your being.
it grows
with courage
— mine and yours

wisdom's light

the light of wisdom flares
awakening your heart
rousing your mind
illuminating your spirit
revealing your purpose

stillness

stillness reverberates
in my soul
awakening wisdom
that must be shared
with the world

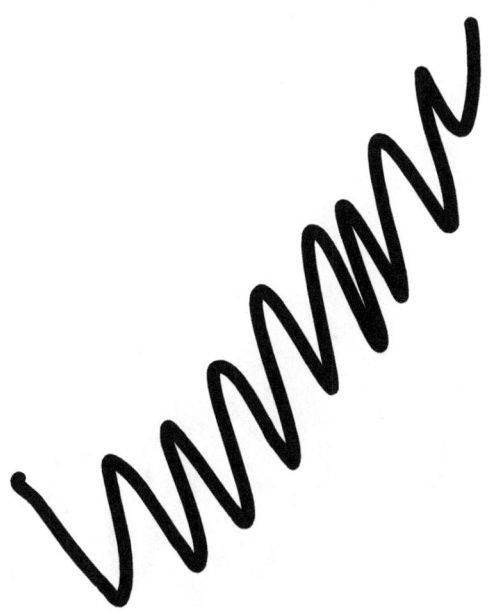

echoing truth

the stillness
of our heart
shares
an echoing truth
not in grand gestures
but simply by
who we are

the sun rises

the sun rises
not to give beauty
to the day
but to shine light
on the beauty
of the day

you are ready

your light
is bright.
it shines
in ways unrecognizable.
the time here.
shout out
with courage,
with love,
with joy.
the time
is coming.
you are ready.

the last puzzle piece

epiphany:
that moment
the last puzzle piece
clicks into place
you understand

a sirocco wind

a sirocco wind
whips through life
picking up
the debris of illusion
leaving the potential
of the real
in its wake.

the cracks in your soul

your heart
knows the answer.
it whisper-twines
from the cracks
in your soul.

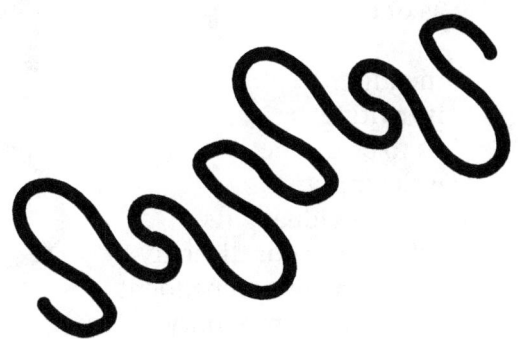

inky blackness

the night
is calling,
rest in
my velvet darkness
know me
listen
with your ears
to the sounds
of my inky blackness

the night
is dancing,
move to
the rhythm
feel how
i come alive
with iridescent sparkleys
flashing in my dark

the night
is living
with each breath
i take
expanding in wisdom
contracting with
understanding
joining us together
as one

the night
is inviting
us to be as one
welcoming
our individual gifts
celebrating our diversity
becoming interdependent
becoming community

my cocoon

to my cocoon:
thank you for
your silken beauty,
your warm protection
as I grew into this person
strong enough to rip a hole
in your beauty

on the ledge

open
the window
sit on the ledge
of your soul
feel the breeze
breathe deeply
leap into
transformation

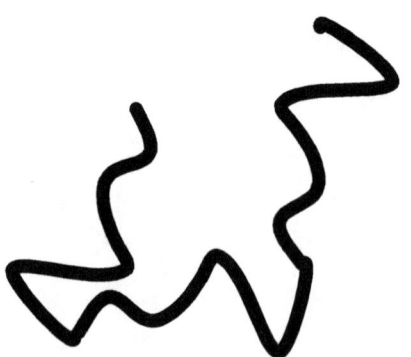

stand up

if you don't
stand up
for yourself
who will?

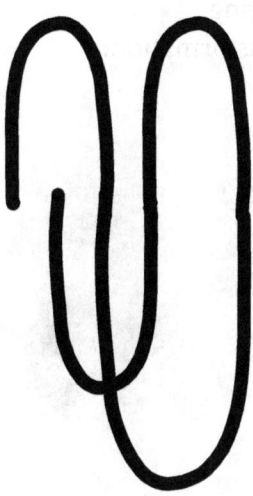

my soul song

within my soul
is a song,
a lamentation
of sorrow,
a melody
of joy,
a whisper
of hope.
within my soul
is a song,
singing
transformation.

not yet time

not yet time
to unfurl your wings.
things are changing
breath in your fear
exhale your courage
inch closer and closer.
prepare.
the time is not yet
to unfurl your wings.
transformation comes

an internal response

we can change
the world
by being
our self
or the uncertainty
of the world
will change us
being the change
is an internal response
to the external world

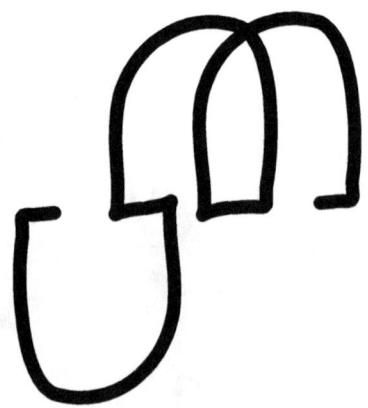

you are gift

you are gift
a pollinator
of peace
a carrier
of compassion
a grower
of gratitude
you are gift
lighting
the dark
blowing away
the stale
preparing
the fallow ground
you are gift

open to magic

open your soul
within it
are your dreams.
open your heart
within it
is your potential.
open your mind
within it
is your possibility.
open your eyes
for within your vision
is magic

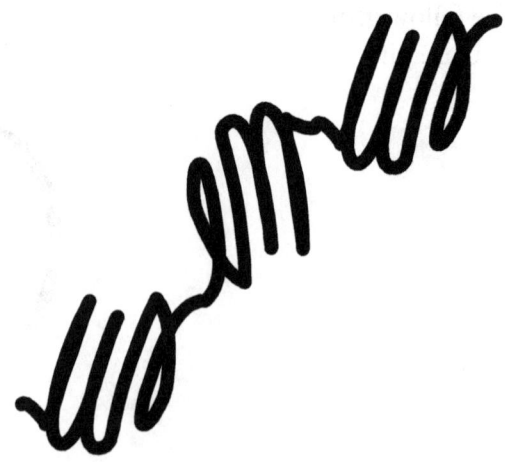

a reminder

within the silence
of my soul
a tattoo beats strong
calling me
into myself
beating hope's rhythm
reminding me
to share my good

an unexpected stem

hope is
an unexpected stem
shooting from your soul
unfurling a flower
of a species unknown

a bird in the dark

a bird sings
in the dark
unseen yet heard.
beauty resonates
in the song.
hope is like that

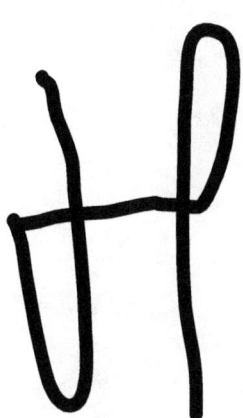

belonging

belonging
sometimes
looks nothing
like you
ever thought
it would
change
your perception
your expectations
you fit
you belong

birthed from my truth

the moon
is dark
so am i
hidden in
plan sight
yearning for
illumination
birthed from
the shadows into
my truth

welcome home

falling
from the east
a lone star
casts shards of light
unto a dark land
welcoming
me home

spiraling into life

this journey is not
a straight shot
from birth to death.
we spiral into life
with known
and unknown
consequences.

sometimes i forget

sometimes,
I forget
that within me
is a spark
so bright
that it blinds
the world
with compassion.
i bet,
sometimes,
you forget
about that spark
inside of you, too.

a fierce heart

a fierce heart
rides on the winds
of curiosity,
courageously
seeding
hope in its wake

take flight

pluck
your deepest desire
from the down
of you soul
stretch the wings
of your heart
take flight
into the sun
of possibility
believe
in your potential

truth whispers

within the silence
truth whispers
welcoming me
into myself
enveloping me
with grace
opening me
to wisdom
sparking
my courage
within the silence
truth whispers

a grace tattoo

open
to the grace
beating a tattoo
in your soul
it powers
your transformation

the stars twinkle

your moment
to shine
is every moment.
the stars twinkle
every night,
don't they?

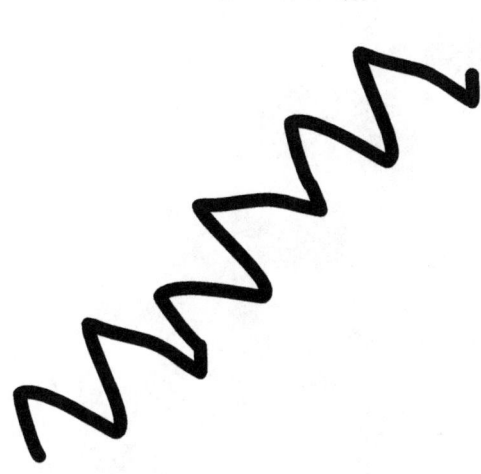

a welcome

the way
is narrow
with dizzying dips,
hairpin turns,
steep climbs.
the way
is narrow
with the most
beautiful vistas
welcoming you
into your self

deserving

you may say,
"i'm not ready.
i'll wait until
i am deserving."

i say,
"you are deserving,
now.
you are ready.
soar."

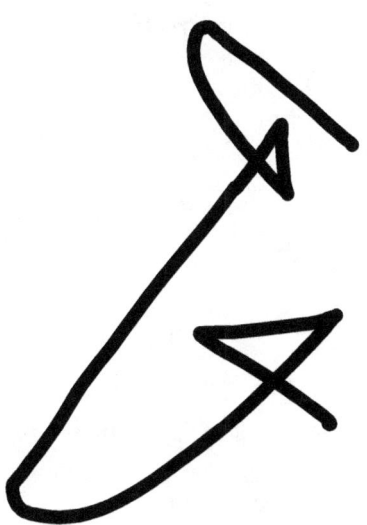

open your eyes

i see you
the brilliance
of your beauty
the honesty
of your truth
the wonder
of your grace
i see you
open your eyes
see yourself

grow your dream

stretch to the sky
root into the earth
today is the day
be your best,
most real self
today is the day
for the power
of your truth
to course
through you
grow your dream

an expression of truth

i love
not because
i can
but because
i must
my love
is the expression
of my truth

love awakens

love awakens
drifting from cracks
in your soul
touching the world
love awakens
seeping into cracks
of your soul
healing the residue
of suffering

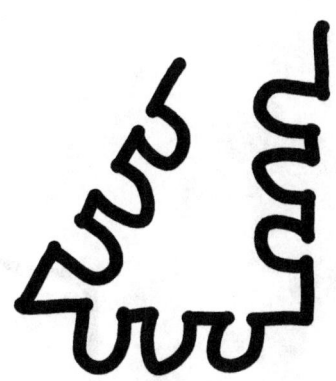

your superpower

your superpower,
your ability to be yourself
and share that truth
with the world

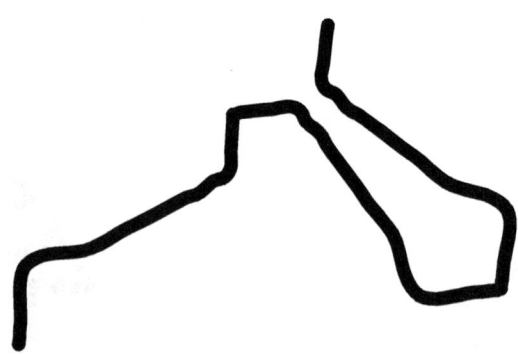

start simple

you don't
have to do it all
at once
start simple
watch yourself grow

the path of your dreams

with each breath
the magic in your soul
flares an aurora borealis
of possibility
revealing the true path
of your dreams.

the scent of possibility

listen
to the beat
of your heart
follow its rhythm
breath in
the scent
of possibility
don't doubt
you got this

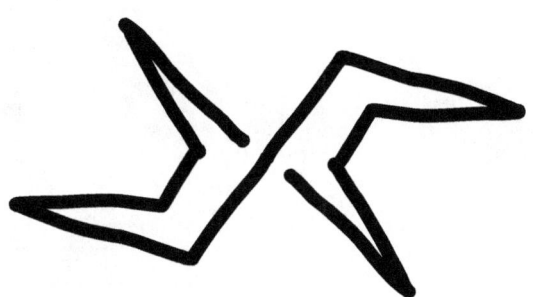

the truth within

the brightness
of the sun
casts shadows
in our soul.
the heat
of the sun
invites us
to explore
the shadows
discovering
the truth
within.

each movement

stretch.
twist.
reach.
realign.
the seeds
of transformation
are planted
in each movement
stretch.
twist.
reach.
realign.

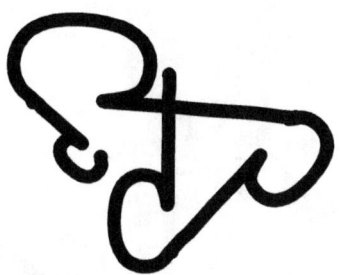

a single raindrop

one single raindrop
of trust
falls upon
your parched soul-ground
moistening the soil
waking the seed of hope

an ill fit

too much,
too little.
it is the situation,
not you,
that doesn't fit.
you are enough
as you are.

are you scared?

are you scared?
so am i.
let's not get lost
in the fog of fear.
hold my hand.
i'll take yours.
combined courage
creates action.
we'll navigate
this uncertainty
together.

i love you enough

i love you enough
the battle cry of a compassion
warrior

i love you enough
sitting in the silence
holding your hand
listening to you weep

i love you enough
hearing beneath your words
feeling your anger
witnessing your frustration

i love you enough
reverberating with your angst
wrestling with my want to repair
recognizing your strength

i love you enough
being compassion's presence
promising not to flee, not to fix
celebrating your wisdom
i love you enough
i am compassion's warrior

boogiemen

step into
your shadows.
the only boogiemen
are festering illusions
grown in the belief
of your failure.

unwrapping into the world

gather
your gifts,
the essence
of who you are,
unwrap them
into the world.

pulsing hope

my heart
beats a fierce tattoo
drumming with courage,
gently pulsing hope
into a wounded world

our true nature

fear is
the ultimate transformer
we can cower
in the dark
never knowing
its name
or we power
courageously
through the dark
discovering
our true nature.

your soul song

reach for the sky
hold it gently
with your eyes
sink into the earth
twine deeply
into the roots
listen to the call
sing from your soul
in response

feeling is believing

open yourself
to the flow
of intuition
feeling is
believing

the night speaks

the night
speaks to me.
the stars
twinkling possibility.
the clouds
casting illusions.
the shadows
sing mystery.
the night
speaks to me.
i listen
i hear
i respond

breathe in the world

breathe in
the world
with your eyes
feel the secrets
bounding
just out of sight
each breath
brings potential
breathe in
change

life happens

life happens
one precious breath
at a time
inhale the wild
exhale the fierce
that's the rhythm
of transformation

seeing-being

a tsunami of grief
washes over you
wakening you
to the poignancy
of loss
don't hold on
to what
can never be
celebrate
grief changes
your landscape
provides a new way
of seeing-being

a humanity reminder

grief
wells up
from our being
not to destroy
but to remind us
of our humanity

the spirit yearns

the spirit
yearns
to be
set free

the eyes of adversity

look deeply
into the eyes
of adversity.
courageously call
its name.
navigate
the path
of challenge.
find hope
in each obstacle
overcome.

no matter

no matter where
no matter how
no matter what
i will not stop
being who i am
from my core
i will not stop
being me

your beauty

be fierce
be kind
shine your light
the world needs
your beauty

grief whispers

grief whispers,
i am not here to stay
i am a realization
loss is inevitable.
i am a testament
to your strength,
your courage,
your compassion

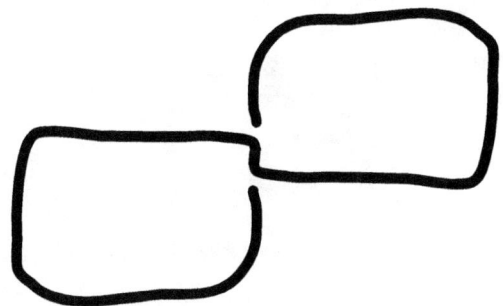

a tsunami of change

courageously ride
the tsunami of change
to peaceful beaches
forever transformed
by your strength,
your resilience

inevitable

remember
change is inevitable
transformation is not.

never fear

never fear
a world
too big,
too uncertain.
you make
a difference.
bring a change
in the little moments
that build
the big

no question

no question
is unanswered.
ask it.
listen intently.
the response echoes
in your world
until you hear it.

you are magic

magic is
in the air.
can you feel it?
swirling up
from you being,
rousing your power,
being change.
magic is
in the air.
it is you.

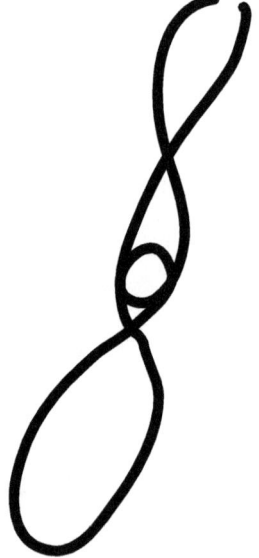

be your power

stand up.
speak out.
be your power.
be you

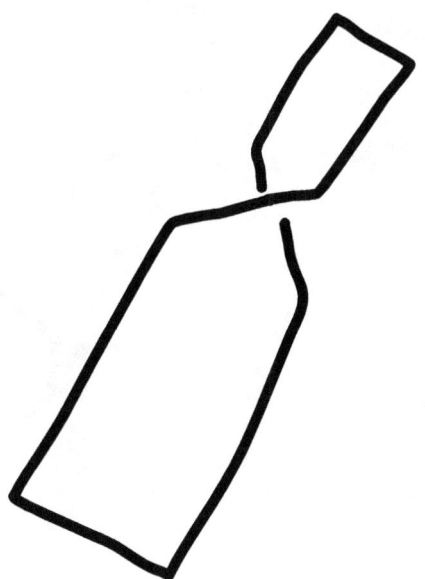

lightning strikes

a lightning strike
of suffering
awakens compassion
in my soul.
igniting fierce beauty
to share with the world

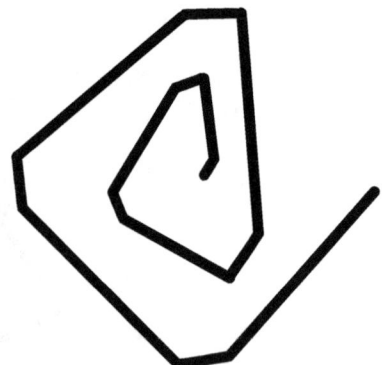

world needs

the world needs
your gentle fierceness
your feral heart
your limitless courage
the world needs you

without power

love fiercely
live courageously
be your unapologetic best

dawn whispers

the sun rises,
dawn whispers,
"wake, wake
to your true self."

within your soul

open your heart
reach within your soul
spark a wildfire
of transformation
with your core

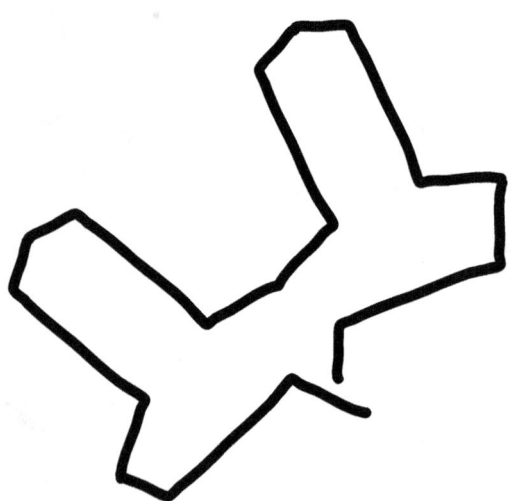

kindling dreams

transformation begins
with the kindling
of your dreams.
transformation begins
with the acknowledgement
of your dreams
transformation begins
with your courageous heart

i ride

i ride
through the margins,
crossing the border
into a time of fierce,
fearless, determined living
of soul purpose.

gather kindling

gather
the kindling
of possibility
light it with
potential's flame
be the truth
you are

slipping through cracks

you are grace
slipping through
the worn cracks
of the world
sharing the beauty
of your spirit

stretch to the sky

stretch
to the sky,
open
your arms,
reach
for your new.
share
your beauty,
your grace,
your fierce being

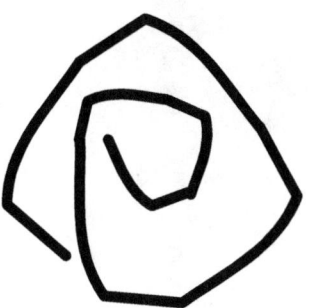

be the response

be **response**
to a world fatigued
by **reaction**!

pilgrimage

pilgrimage
a journey of lighting
your sacred spark.

so do i

the sun rises
so do i
burning off
the fog of uncertainty
transforming suffering
into learning
revealing
beauty within the scars
the sun rises
so do I

ride the thermal

change
is coming
believe it
breathe it
ride the thermal
of transformation
into your dreams

find peace

may you
find peace
in the quiet smiles,
the gentle laughter,
the simple joys
of the day

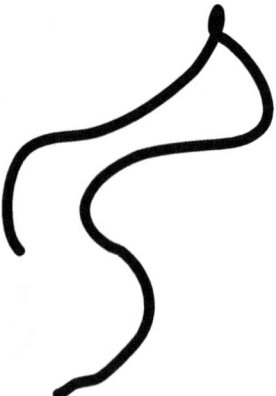

the night is quiet

the night
is quiet
no moon
to light your way
the stillness speaks
demanding
to be seen
paint
the aurora borealis
of your soul
on your blank canvas
the night
is quiet
you light
your way

a thin place

in this thin place
peer softly
through the veil
breathe in
the wisdom
make it
your own
accept
who you are

the abyss of possibility

open your heart
bare your soul
soften your gaze
peer with the entirety
of your being
into the abyss
of possibility

my truth revealed

the whispers
of my spirit
open the veil
of my soul
revealing
my truth

are you ready?

dawn edges
across the horizon
a new day
a new way.
are you ready?
i am.

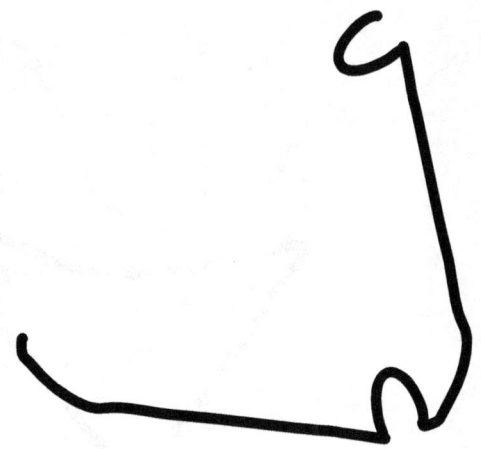

you thrive

your light
shines brightest
when you believe
in yourself
this belief opens
a gateway to magic
enter this mystery place
thrive within its magic

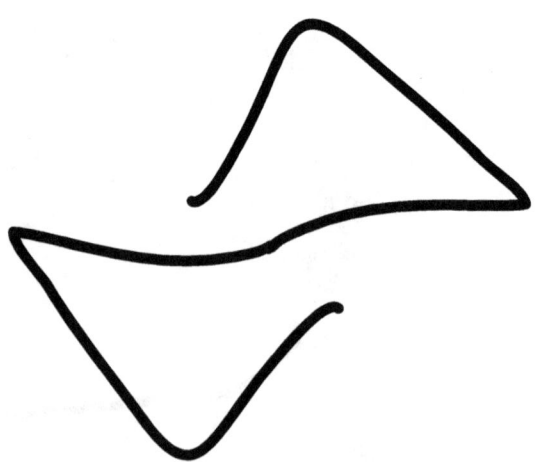

lit from within

the light
that shines within
is kindled by
your truth
ignited by
your connection
to all

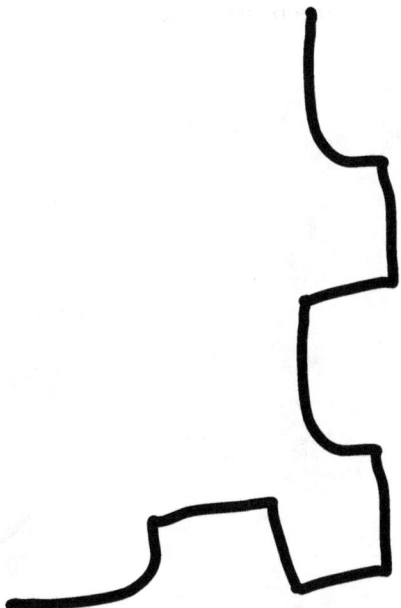

seeds

each ending
seeds
a beginning
toss your seeds
one more time

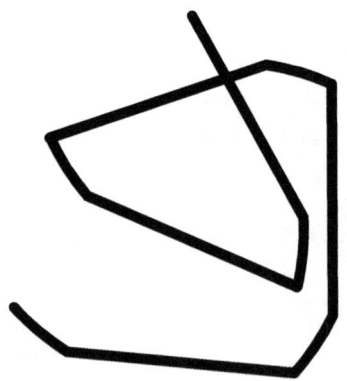

blind illusion

be the light
that blinds illusions
bringing forth
your truth

a dream yearns

a dream
yearns
to burst forth
believe in
your dream
it guides you
through life

mystery whispers

mystery whispers,
"take my hand,
follow my lead,
through the shadows
into the place
where your magic sparks
transformation

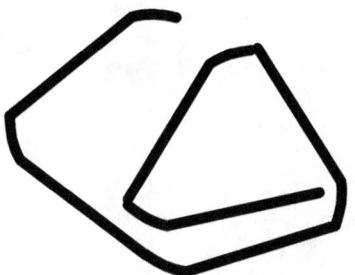

i am grace

i am grace
resonating
wisdom beyond knowing,
courageous truth,
fierce beauty.
finally woke to who i am.

from the mud

i am
a seed
bursting forth
from the mud.
a twining healer
of myself
and worlds.
i am gift.

one more

don't stop
climb
one more step
open
one more door
reach out to
one more person
live with purpose
share yourself
the world needs you
as you are

awakened inspiration

your spirit wakens
to the cold patter of rain
seeping through the cracks
of your soul
awakening inspiration

dark to light

dark to light
light to dark.
let go.
breathe through.
clarity comes
from understanding.
deep inside
you know

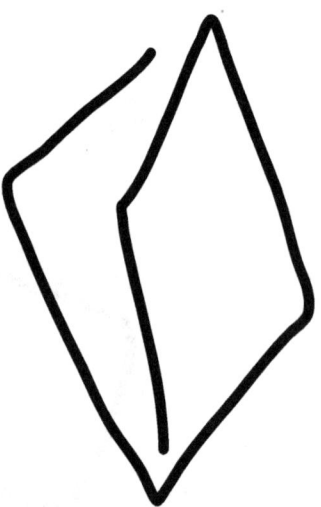

grief's triad

grief awakens
strength,
resilience,
persistence.
grief calls forth
your true self
grief resonates
gratitude for the past
joy in the present
hope of the future

chaos ricochet

chaos:
a ricochet of reaction
wearing down the barriers
of what no longer works
revealing glimpses
of the new

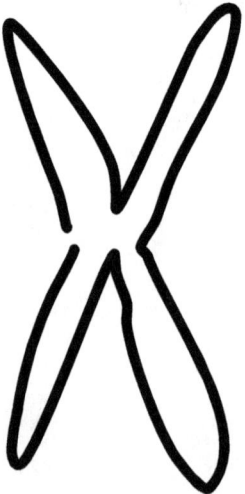

without

be yourself
without condition
love yourself
without reserve
share yourself
without fear
act from the depth
of your soul
that is all
that is enough

a whisper of promise

a whisper
of promise
is found
in each moment
of gratitude.

enough

shine your light
be your truth
share your grace
that is your enough

silence waits

silence
waits
for us
to listen

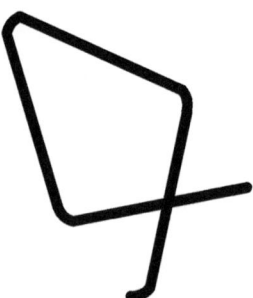

hope thrives

hope
doesn't thrive
in the absence
of suffering
it grows
with each act
of compassion
received
… and given

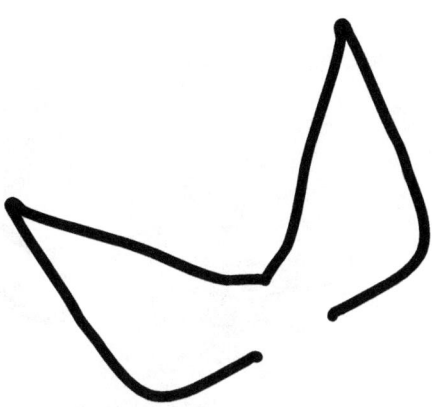

the greatest gift

give yourself
the greatest gift:
belief in yourself,
your abilities,
believe in the possibility
to change yourself
…and the world.

scatter seeds

scatter seeds
grow roots
soar into the sky
spark into the stars
shine into the sun
be the grace
you dream for the world

no container

within you
is a beauty, a grace,
that cannot, will not,
be contained.
share it

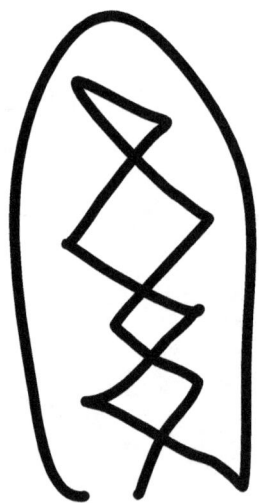

like a fierce storm

like a fierce storm
suffering swirls
around you
cleansing you
making you whole

in the stillness

in the stillness
of the morning
breathe in calm
soothe your fears
greet the day

in the stillness
of the morning
breath out peace
gentle rough edges
be resilient change

in the stillness
of the morning
breathe into yourself
breathe out in anticipation

be a beacon

the fullness
of the moon
reflects the truth
of who you are.
shine your light.
be a beacon
in a world gone dark.

arms wide open

open your arms
gather in the wisdom
of your spirit
share the beauty
of your heart
have courage
to be your dream

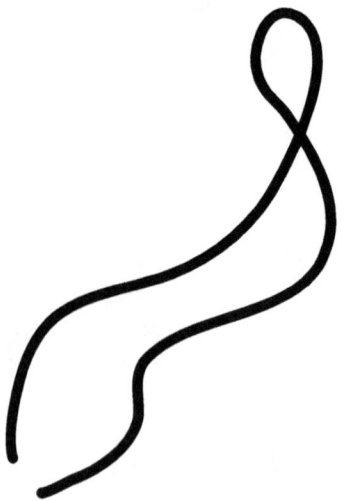

a power so great

within you
is a power
so great
it cannot
be denied.
be who you know
you are.

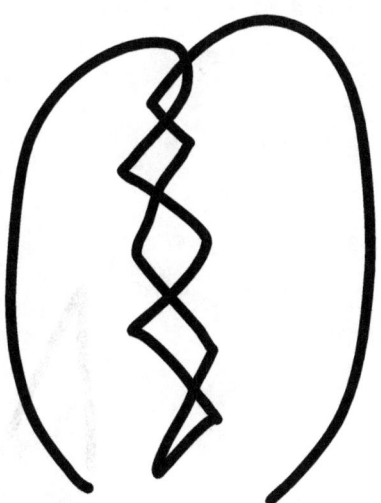

a quiet hush

you are
more expansive
more courageous
more powerful
than you realize
believe
be

you are the world

the night
whispers, "rest"
its quiet hush
wraps us in hope
soothes our suffering
reveals the beauty within

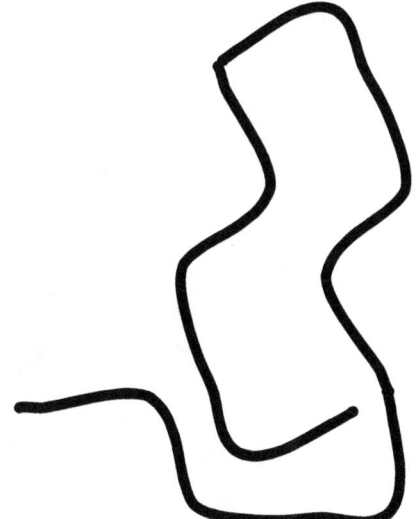

the longest night

the world
doesn't revolve
around you.
you are the world.
your thoughts,
your words,
your actions
brighten its light
…or dims it.

sacred calm

the hush
of the longest night
wraps around you
igniting the truth
within the sacred calm,
you find yourself

yearning

within my heart
is a yearning
so sharp
it must be answered.

to answer the yearning
is to transform.

in transformation,
i become
who i always was.

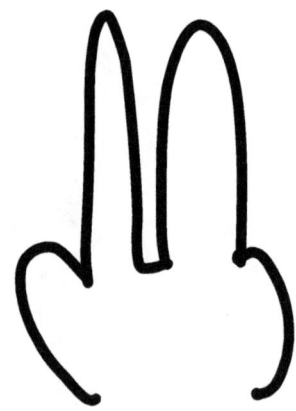

a flickering candle

that flickering candle
in the dark
is you

seamlessly flow

let go
seamlessly flow
wake up
be who you are

believe

believe in
your compassion,
your integrity,

believe in
the beauty of your soul,
the kindness of your heart.

believe in
your courage,
your strength to try
one more time

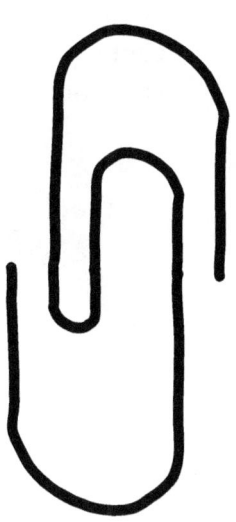

birthing

i am
the chaser
of illusions
the revealer of truth
that you are strong,
courageous,
grace filled.

i am the birther
of your soul wisdom,
your heart compassion.

i am your truth.
i am you.

disappointment

disappointment is
an opportunity to
reassess,
realign,
and recommit

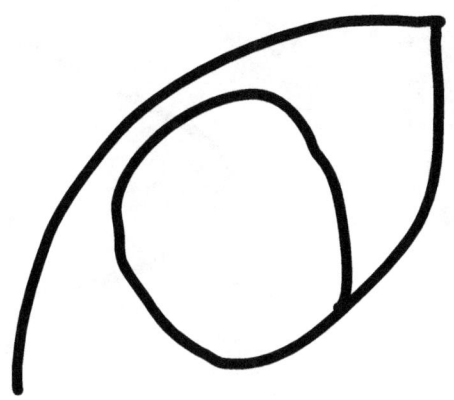

a barren land

you are
the light
transforming
a barren land
into dreams realized.

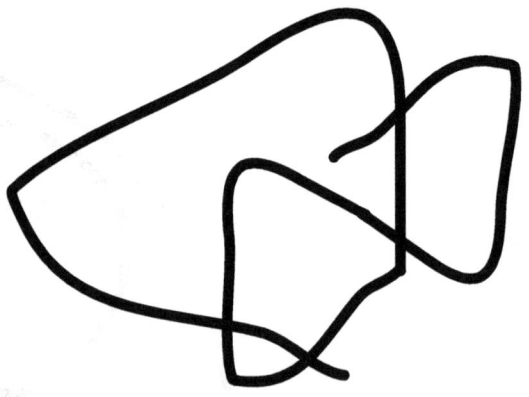

scatter hope

scatter your hopes
into the world
believe in the potential
of your dreams
live as if there is
enough for all

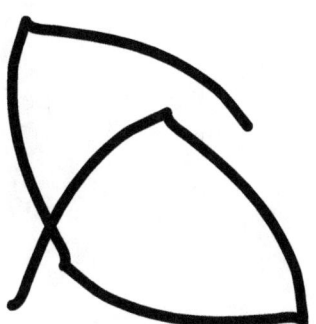

my absurd reaction

i woke up laughing
not at the absurdity
of the world
but by my absurd reaction
to it.

unimaginable love

a love
unimaginable
seeped out
from my heart
changing me
forever

a lotus blossom

within me
is a joy so great
it cannot be contained.
like a lotus blossom,
it bursts through
the murky depths
of my being
unfolding its beauty
into a imperfect world.

too fast to hear

a whisper roars.
you are dancing
too fast to hear.
slow down.
trust the melody
is here.

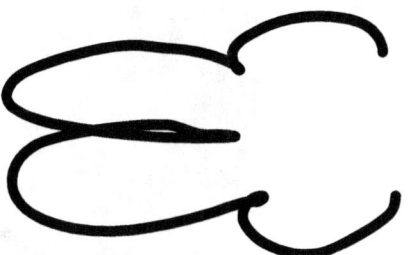

change is coming for you

a gentle breeze,
a hot sirocco wind,
a hurricane gale.
listen.
let go.
change is coming
for you.

your birthright

reach for the stars
the dust of creation,
the ancient beginnings
of your birthright.

the way is simple

do you want
to change the world?
the way is simple:
be who you are.

freedom laughs

freedom laughs
at the illusion
of your captivity
freedom breathes
into the staleness
of your soul
freedom awakens
the fierce rebel
of your spirit

i laughed

when i discovered
my way through
i laughed.
it seemed
too easy
to be true,
but it was.
easy and true

A rejection, a correction

a rejection
is a correction
in your life path
listen to the radar
of your intuition
pinging you
on the true path

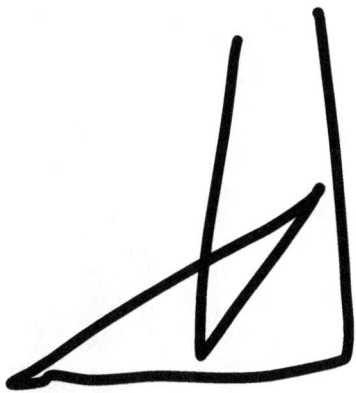

courage up

courage up
courage out
stand up
stand out
speak up
speak out
it's time

your greatest act

believe that
you deserve
this is
your greatest act
of compassion

be the breeze

ruffle feathers,
crinkle leaves,
blow dandelion fluff.
be the breeze
bringing freshness,
to a grieving world.

accept responsibility

accept responsibility
…for what is yours

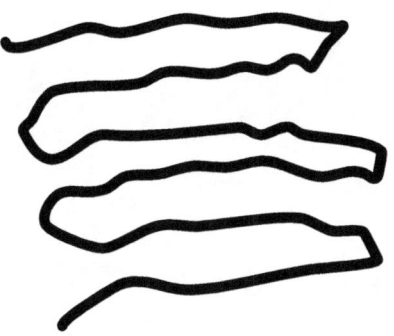

everlasting

within you is
a fierce strength
An everlasting compassion
a power unknown

within you is
a letting go
a gentle call
a new beginning

within you is a
spark of wisdom
a feral spirit
a whisper that shouts truth

renewal

breathe in.
the newness of the day
sparks a wildfire of renewal.

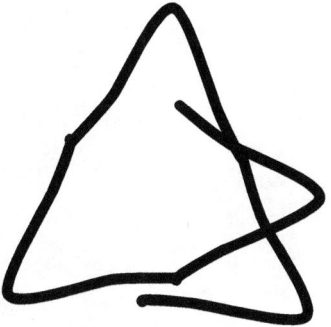

friend or foe

fear can be a friend
revealing our courage.
fear can be a foe
blocking our purpose.

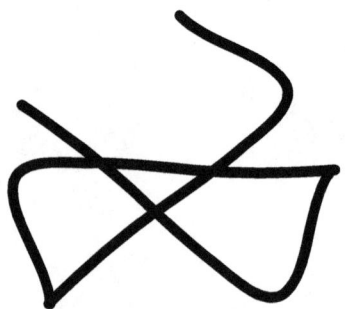

don't

don't give up.
don't give in.
name your fear
call upon your courage.
love your self.
shine from your core.

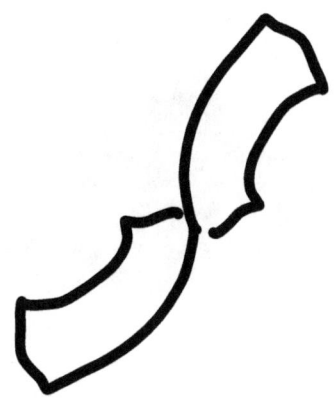

as close as letting go

the answer
is as close
as letting go.
open your heart.
open your mind.
trust your soul.
free fall into the answer.

so bright

within you is
a spark so bright,
so powerful,
so awesome
it ignites
the belief in
your self

you resist

the answer
is easy,
yet,
you resist
its simplicity.

a fierce soul

a fierceness
in your soul
longs
to be set free
breathe
in the wonder
of the moment
breathe out
your daring
step forward
with curiosity
move through
with courage

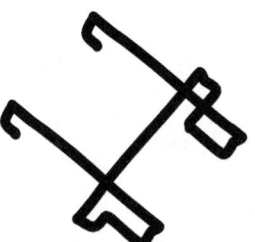

your power

you have the power
to change the world
by changing your self

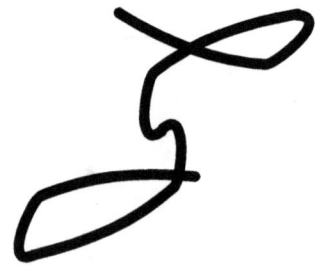

what stops you

let go
of what
stops you
from
being whole

it is you

breathe in.
rise up.
change is coming.
it is you.

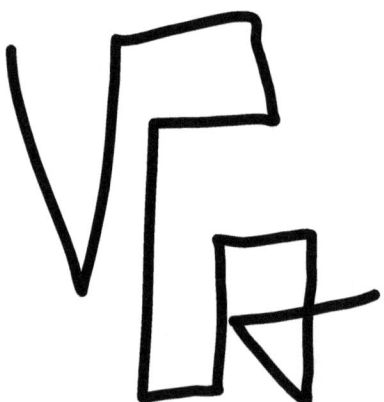

be real

let go of
what stops you
from being real

embrace

let go
of who you think
you are
embrace who
you are

the end of the tunnel

you are the light
at the end
of your tunnel.

no shame

hold on tight
to your hopes.
your dreams,
your purpose.
there is no shame.
hold on tight.
it's not over
until you let go.

don't. give. up.

don't. give. up.
dream your big dream.
believe in your grand gift
make the dream,
the gift
as real as you.

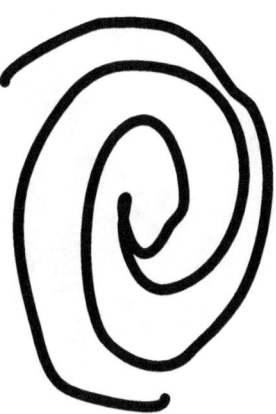

the time is nigh

awake
from your slumber
the time is nigh
turn your head
to the east,
the north,
the south
breathe deep
the time is nigh

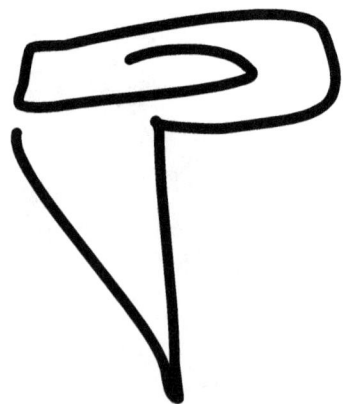

open your soul

an open mind,
an open heart,
opens your soul

accept

accept
that you deserve
accept
what you deserve

saying no

saying no is
knowing,
trusting,
believing
that as
one door closes
another opens

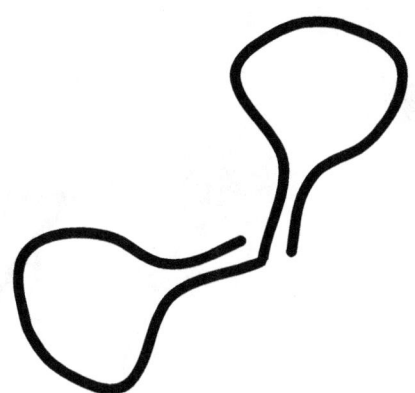

channel courage

speak your truth
share your power
channel your courage
now, more than ever,
the world needs you

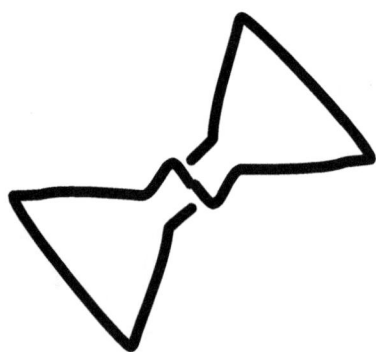

the sand is shifting

the sand is shifting
not to swallow me
but to change
my perception
of me
and the world

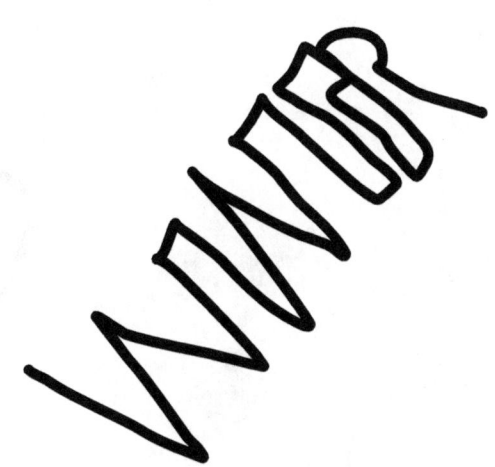

greatness

the fear gestating
in your soul
does not paralyze
it propels you
to greatness

bear witness

be the light
that bears witness
in the dark

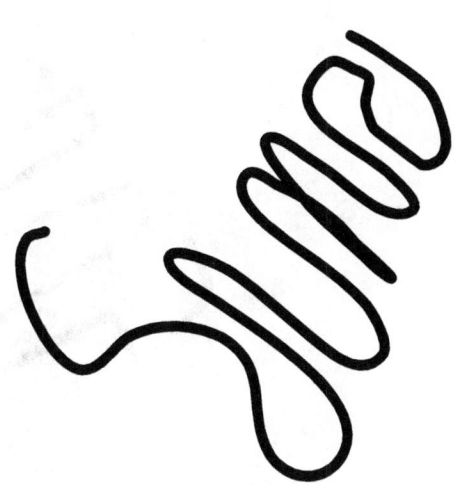

within chaos

within chaos
is a peace so profound
it changes you
on a soul level

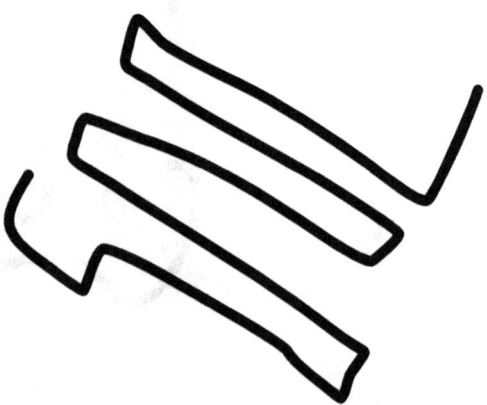

live fierce

to be yourself
is to live
from the fierceness
of your heart

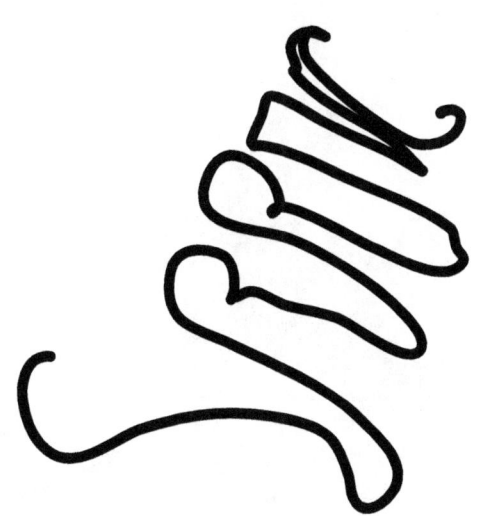

a way forward

look not for
a way out
but a way forward

a little bit lost

to find
your way
befriend
the part
of yourself
that is
a little bit
lost

untapped power

the universe has
a fierce,
untapped power
that releases
each time
you breathe
deeply
into your soul
igniting
the spark within

the moon casts light

even if
the sun
has set
on your dreams
the moon
casts light
to guide
your way

pointing toward

hope
is an arrow
pointing toward
the way
of soul purpose.

hope
is believing
possibility
is birthed
from your purpose

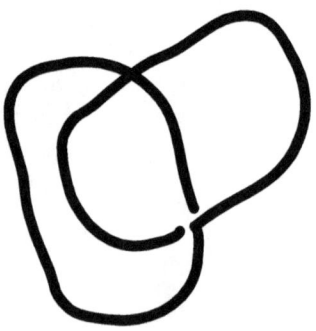

five letters

maybe
five letters
that bring us
 to the heights
of hope
or plunge us
into the depths
of despair
maybe

beginning anew

the birds
are singing
reminding me
each day
begins anew
and so do I

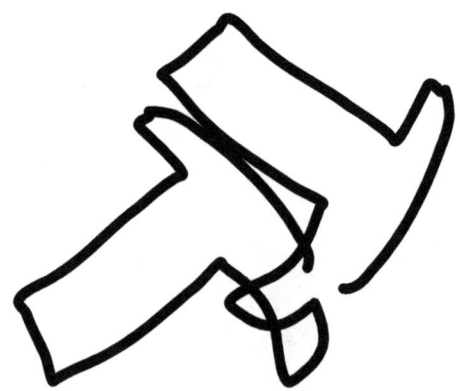

over my soul

dawn washes
over my soul
reminding me,
one more time,
to be myself.

in yourself

the greatest,
most profound belief
you will ever have
is the belief in yourself

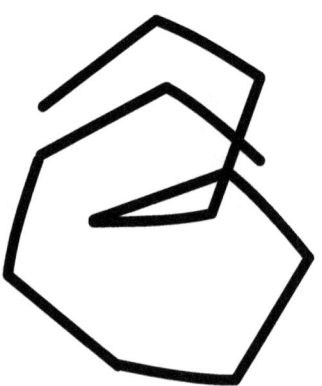

living acceptance

transformation is
not changing
who you are.
transformation is
accepting
who you are
transformation is
living
that acceptance.

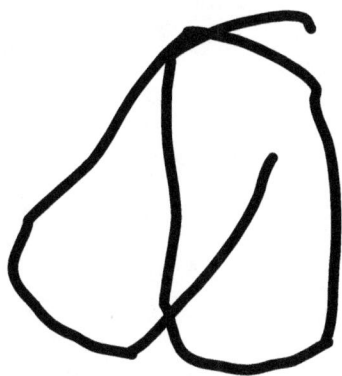

eyes open

how can
you navigate
the path
with your eyes
closed?

forgiveness

your path is lit
by forgiveness
of yourself

winds of letting go

the winds of letting go
clear the clouds of
shoulda,
woulda,
coulda.
the clearing sky
twinkles
with limitless
possibilities

echo of truth

within each pause
is an echo
of your truth
waiting to speak
within each heartbeat
is the voice
of your truth

just because

just because
the path is unclear
doesn't mean it isn't there.

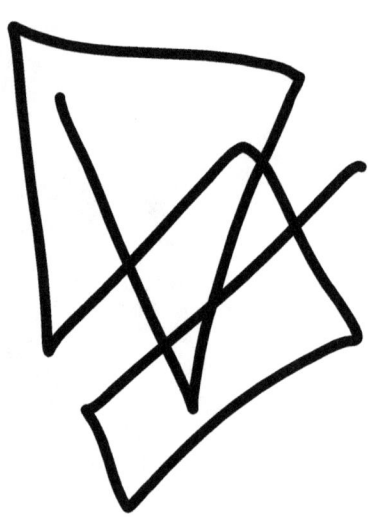

of magic

belief in yourself is
the when
the where
the how
of magic

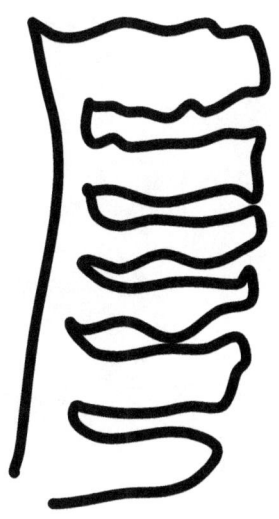

conquer

within moments
of grace
you conjure mystery
you call upon magic
you conquer yourself

never enough

in a bid
to be enough,
we create
a monstrous cycle
of never enough.

got something

when you
"got nothing,"
you are so deep
in the pause
unable to
fully identify
possibilities.
breathe.
listen.
you've got
something
it is hidden
in the shadows
of your soul

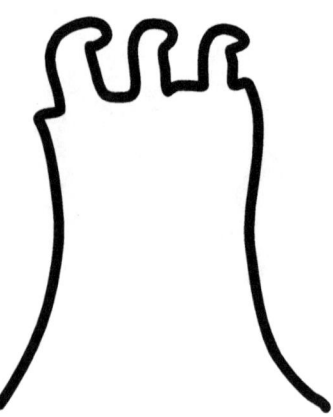

two choices

when the ledge
begins to crumble,
you have
two choices
fall…
or fly

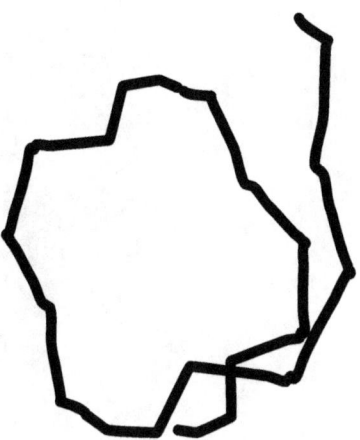

become the sky

to realize
your dreams,
do not reach
for the sky.
become the sky.

the winds blow

i don't know
where the winds blow
i only know
they speak to me
of hope
of change
of transformation
soar onto a thermal
dare to become yourself

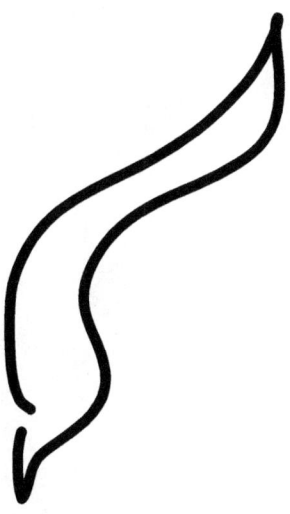

uncertainty unraveled

the power
of your dreams
unravel the uncertainty
in your soul

guiding me home

i know where the wind blows
it blows deep in my soul
igniting a wildfire of passion
revealing the path of purpose
guiding me home

set free

listen
to the beauty
of your soul
it sets you free

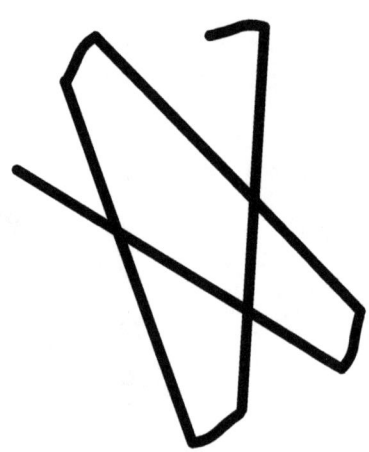

shining within

the light
that shines
the brightest
is the light
that shines within

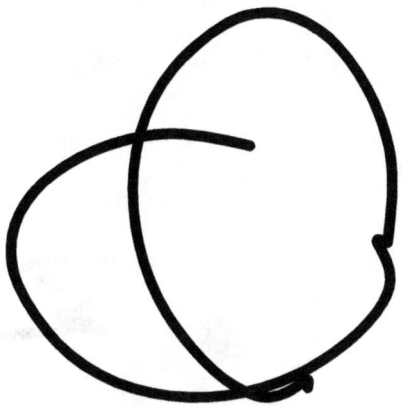

falling leaves

the falling leaves
do not herald endings
they reveal the beginnings
echoing in our hearts

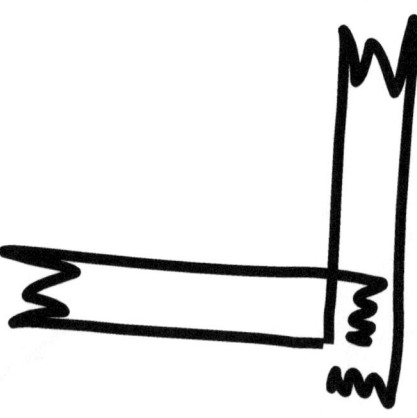

not your foe

your fear is
not your foe
it is a voice
of intuition
guiding you
through
the paralysis
of dark
into the light
of action.

the power of dreams

the power
of your dreams
cast light
on the fear
in your heart
& unravel
the uncertainty
in your soul

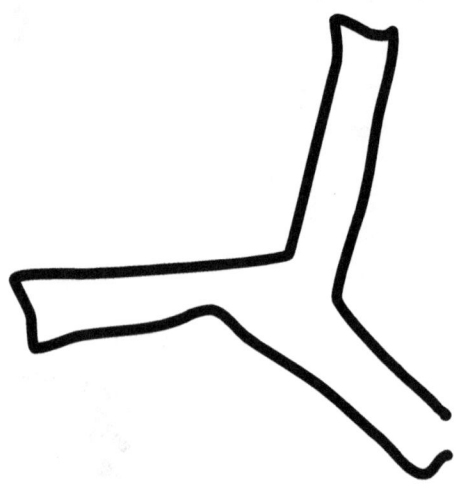

the whisper of free

listen
to the beauty
of your soul
it seeks
to set
you free

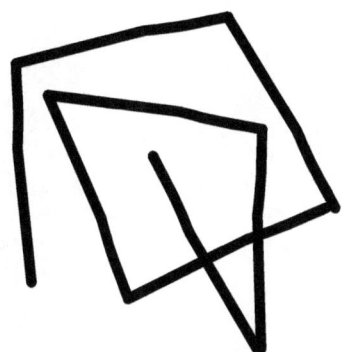

free to be

i am free
free to speak
from my soul
free to act
from my heart
free to believe
in possibility
free to be
unapologetically me

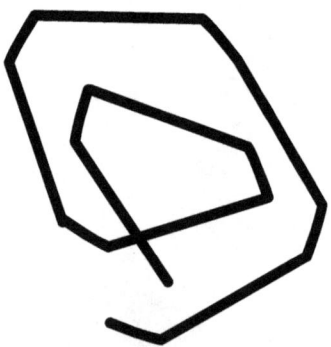

really awake

are you awake?
really awake.
the kind of awake
that has you knowing
exactly who you are

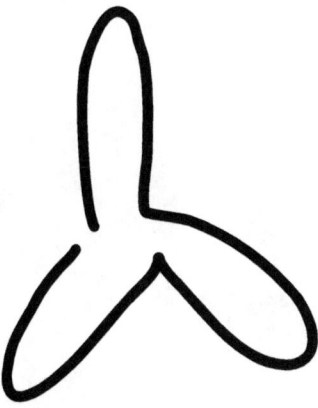

bright enough

your light is
bright enough
to find the way
through the shadows
cast by doubt,
fear, uncertainty
your brilliance ignites
a darkened path

believe in

believe in
the wisdom
of your soul
believe in
the clarity
of your vision
believe in
the quiet,
still voice
calling you
home
to yourself

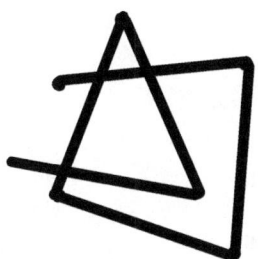

into the unknown

sometimes
the only thing
you can do
is let go
and catch
a thermal
into the unknown.

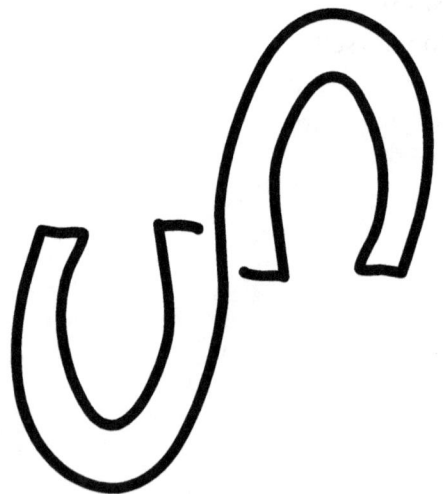

the night is not over

breathe deep,
breathe fierce
reignite your light
chase the dark
the night is not over
neither are you

anyone but yourself

you do not
have to be
anyone
but yourself.

it's not about

it's not about
reaching
for the stars.
it's about
reaching into
the darkness
at your core
to nurture
the spark
within

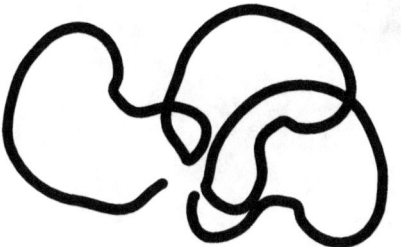

no more detours

no more detours
just path corrections
leading me
to my self

becoming whole

stomp your feet
gnash your teeth
cry those ugly tears
grieve it out
in purging your soul
you become whole

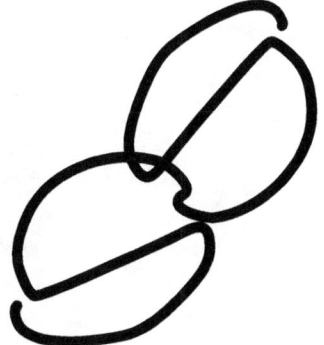

ask the question

you are
the answer
you have
been waiting for.
ask the question.

true to you

be fierce.
be unapologetic.
be true to you.
whatever you believe in,
believe first
in yourself.

no matter how dark

the moon dances
in and out
of the clouds
playing
hide and seek
with my soul
reminding me
no matter
how dark
the night,
my light
always shines

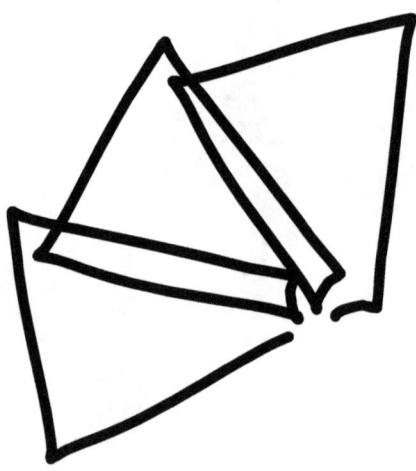

within the shards

my world crashed
within the shards
i discovered the beauty
of what really was.
i smiled.

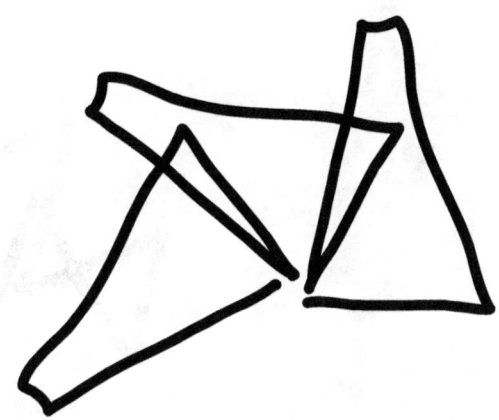

may you

may your spirit
dance lightly
upon the earth
may you find joy
in the little moments
may you walk
between the worlds
may you shine
from the center
of your being

mystery

life is mystery
a walk into the unknown
an inhale of uncertainty
an exhale of wonder

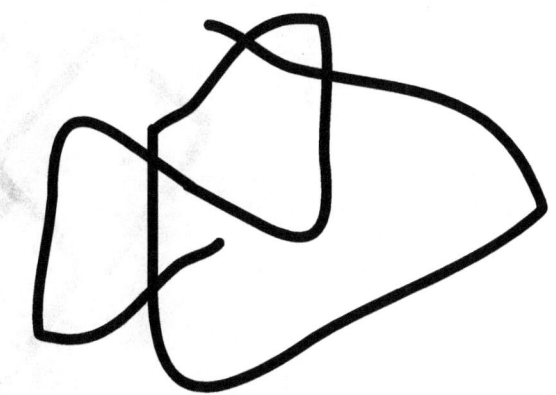

i am expression

i am
the expression of my soul purpose
carried forth
throughout lifetimes
to share my gifts
in this moment

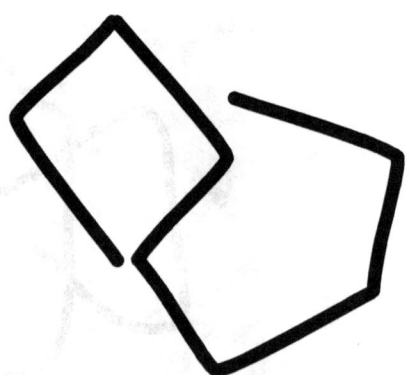

night

in the stillness of the night,
in the quiet of the moment,
in the sacred calm,
we live our truth

Stepping Along Journey's Path

    A journey is never truly over. We walk and walk and walk exploring and rediscovering over and over again what it means to live at this time, in this place — to connect with our self, others, the sacred, and all of creation in ways that give us joy. In this ongoing walk of discovery we refine our path.

    Upon my path, wisdom sparks flourish. This book is but one flower in the sacred bouquet manifest on my journey. I hope that you recognize your flowers and bouquets. I am sure that there are more flowers blossoming into existence. Life doesn't ask us to stop at one blossom, to pluck only wonder from one garden…it asks, "What can we grow during each season of our life? What can we share during all of the seasons?" And, life demands that we discover these answers over and over again.

    With this book, number five, I have finally owned my inner artist. I used to think that I needed to create images to be an artist. Not true — although during Covid, I did begin to paint. Any act of creativity is an ignition sparking of your inner artist. I've also discovered that I needed to start where I found myself. So do you. Create for yourself. That is how I began to write poems and prose. In time I discovered that when I let go of the fear that I wasn't good enough, the words flowed through me. That is what I hope that you discover.

    Want to create poetry? Start with a haiku (first line: 5 syllables, second line: 7 syllables, third line: 5 syllables). Or write something that whispers from your core demanding to be heard. You don't even need to share it with anyone. Hold it close to your heart. Don't toss it away. In time you will grow into the practice. Art speaks from the heart. And, we all need to response more to those heart strands that create the tapestry of your inner artist!

    So, what is next? Perhaps these sparks encourage you to recognize how you show up in each moment. Perhaps you discover how the sacred weaves through you life. When you recognize how you are showing up and how the sacred shows up, you are living contemplatively.

One last thought: Labels and definitions only work if you create them for yourself — not for others. While we may have similarities on this journey, our relationship with the sacred is magically, uniquely our own. Through these wisdom sparks, I hope that you discover that. In that discovery, I hope that your inner artist shines forth in ways that brighten the world.

Curious to Continue the Contemplative Journey?

As Natural As Breathing: Being Intuitive: invites you to travel the journey of intuitive awareness that began many years ago for me. This book, an affirmation that we are all intuitive, provides a template for discovering that your intuitive abilities are as natural as breathing. Within the covers are the means to move past the fear that prevents you from engaging your intuitive nature. It a recognition that while we all get stuck at some point, through practice we dissolve barriers to our intuition, connect to our inner wisdom, and develop our intuitive presence.

This book is a deep dive into the anatomy of intuition — including the moving along through the intuitive awareness continuum, the role of eight intelligences, our senses, and the nervous system in our ability to engage our intuition. It contains tools and practices to strengthen connection to intuitive awareness.

Imperfect in an Uncertain World: Your Life, Your Message: The world has never been so connected — we communicate instantaneously, watch the world unfolding on 24-hour news channels, and jet thousands of miles away in a matter of hours. Yet, a virus of dissociation rages across the globe. Schisms have formed between nations, political ideologies, and religious beliefs. Deepening schisms need not be the end of our story. Within each of us is the power to bridge these divides and, in doing so, create a compassionate, nonviolent world. How do we begin? By recognizing that we are imperfect in an uncertain world.

This book is a mosaic of nonviolence and compassion wisdom created with tiles fired with knowledge from Thomas Merton,

Dorothee Soelle, Mahatmas Gandhi, Marshall Rosenberg, Pema Chödrön, and others. Taking an inward-out approach, Imperfect in an Uncertain World: Your Life, Your Message is a resource for recognizing and minimizing the impact of internal and external violence in your life. Through a series of practices, name your imperfections, rescript your life, and reframe your reactions to responses. Strengthen your commitment to living imperfectly, nonviolently, and compassionately in an uncertain world.

A Constellation of Connections: Contemplative Relationships: "I haven't failed, I can tell you 10,000 ways how not to be in relationship." Instead of viewing our relationships in terms of success or failure, this book offers a relationship paradigm shift. Shifting from a winning or losing relationship paradigm, our connections with others become opportunities to experience our challenges, learn our life lessons, and meet our life purpose. By reframing the way we perceive relationships, we create more mindful, contemplative connections with our self, others, the sacred, and all of creation.

This book uses the image of the night sky as a metaphor for living mindfully in relationship. The darkness of the sky is silence, the environment in which our awareness flourishes in real time. The twinkling stars reflect the sparks of compassion present within each of us. Communion, the connector of our constellation, forms through intentional listening and compassionate response. Through silence, compassion, and communion, our life becomes a constellation of contemplative relationships.

Engaging Compassion Through Intent & Action: Compassion is lived experience — a unique expression of an alleviation of suffering. Being compassionate grows from our intent. But, we get busy; the connection between our intent and action is severed. That not need be the end of the story. Through compassionate response we rebuild and strengthen this connection from intent to action.

This book uses the metaphor of a bridge as a template for reconnecting our intent and action. The bridge has three major components: three foundational awarenesses, four life pillars, and cables of mindfulness practice. Included in the book are experiential activities for creating and sustaining a bridge between intent and action. Create a bridge; shift from fear-filled reaction to compassionate response.

I am Vanessa F Hurst, ms, cmc — a mystic, a contemplative, an intuitive whose life is ignited by the sacred spark within. Opening a window into the extraordinary and sharing that view with others is my passion. I am a spiritual director and a program facilitator of lived experience, an intuitive-contemplative-catalyst, and an artist of aura portraits. I am the author of five books available through wildefyr press (www.wildefyrpress.com) Join me on this journey of self discovery.

www.ingramcontent.com/pod-product-compliance
Lightning Source LLC
Chambersburg PA
CBHW060558170426
43201CB00009B/823